Brain Friendly Guidance Activities To Build Emotional Intelligence

Connie Messina

Editor: Susanna Palomares

Cover: Linda Jean Thille

ISBN: 1-931061-23-8

Jalmar Press
PO Box 370
Fawnskin, CA 92333
Tel: (800) 429-1192(909) 866-2912
Fax:(909) 866-2961
www.jalmarpress.com

Printed in the United States of America

Acknowledgments

It is not often that one gets to publicly thank the people who have impacted his or her life. This book has been a labor of love for me, and I would like thank the following people for their impact on my life and their contributions to this book.

Bobbi DePorter and Joe Chapon of The Learning Forum "Supercamp" program for showing me how to have fun while learning.

Joanne Wall for suggesting that I write a book.

Christine Pare, my former guidance supervisor in the San Diego School District, who taught me the value of prevention and early intervention.

Eric Jensen for his "Brainy" books and trainings, which translate complicated science into a format that we can all understand.

Bradley and Cathy Winch of Jalmar Press for believing in me.

Jeannette Vos and Gordon Dryden for introducing us to "The Learning Revolution."

Susanna Palomares for her patience and skillful editing.

Michael Dove for his wisdom and intuition.

The board members of our nonprofit organization, who have sustained me and contributed to my emotional intelligence: Gus Licht, Antonette Dresser, Phinga Evelyn Kheo, Sharon Bowls, Emma Borens, Gwynne Wady, Jim and Betty Buchanan, Michael Dove, Joanne Stepanchak, Dr. Bret Mosher, Peggy Chana, Ed Duenez, Rose Davis, Ramona Hallam, Scott Marvel, Ronnie Sue Gott, Arlie Neskahi, Marilyn Harryman, and Jeannette Redlich.

My former students, especially those from Abraxas High School and San Diego State University, for laughing at my jokes and expanding their comfort zones with our silly activities. To the Canadian students who traveled to San Diego State University, you are all in my heart. Andrew Madison, you did it!

My colleagues and teachers at San Diego State and the University of San Diego for allowing me to grow as I was teaching others.

Congressman Bob Filner, Judge James Milliken, Nanci Bell and Pat Lindamood, you listened and helped.

My foster son, Christopher Daly, who made me practice what I preached!

John Corcoran, for reminding us that all children can learn to read with proper instruction and properly trained teachers.

Candace Bates-Quinn, illuminator in my life!

Gordon Winder, my friend and my teacher.

My pets, living and departed: Pluto, Heather, Keisha, Molly, Jasmine, Cocoa, Slate, and of course, NiNi; for their unconditional love and faithful companionship.

Most importantly, my mother and father, Rose and Tony Messina, my brothers, Alan Messina and Michael Messina, my sisters, MaryAnn Fagan and Sandi Swanson, my brothers in-law, James Fagan Jr. and Bruce Swanson, and my extended family of aunts, uncles, cousins, nieces and nephews who always taught me the power of love. (It's an Italian thing with us.)

Finally, I would like to acknowledge and thank all of the school counselors who quietly go about their jobs each day helping children and families. Your work is valued and appreciated.

Table of Contents

Introduction

We can put on new shoes, but walk down old paths.

Chinese Proverb

Author and futurist Daniel Quinn states that needed change will come from people with *changed minds* and not from people with new programs. There is no shortage of new programs or curricula on the educational market. Unfortunately, many of them end up sitting on bookshelves, because they don't create "changed minds." In other words, they don't help us to see the need for change or give us the skills to do things differently, and when a new program doesn't bring new results, it is often abandoned.

The purpose of this book is twofold. The first is to provide engaging lessons that teach the very important life skills of Emotional Intelligence, and the second is to encourage teachers and school counselors to experience a "Brain-Friendly" approach to teaching. Whether the lesson is guidance-related or academic, it can be both fun and effective. These lessons work because they touch the heart, and students enjoy them.

Why do we need to change anything?

The real voyage of discovery consists not in seeking new landscapes, but in having new eyes.

Marcel Proust

Our educational system was designed for stability, but the very stability that is advantageous to us in some ways also makes it difficult to implement systemic change. Many of the teaching methods used today target the general population and often don't meet individual needs. Consequently, teachers and, ultimately, school counselors are bombarded with crises arising from disengaged students. Schools are rife with discipline problems and apathy, at the same time as the public is calling for better test results.

Educators, who continually work in a crisis mode "putting out fires" are at risk themselves for burnout from the stress, and worse, that stress gets passed on to the students. Therefore, if we can shift ourselves *within the system* to work "smarter," we will be healthier, happier and more able to achieve the positive results we seek.

Learning specialist and author Eric Jensen states that 75 percent of teachers are sequential, analytic presenters, and 70 percent of all their students do not learn that way. This sets the teacher and the students on a collision course sometimes requiring school counselor intervention. Jensen asserts that many learners who seem apathetic would be very enthusiastic if the learning were offered in their preferred learning style.

The presentation format for the lessons in this book is designed to include all learning styles — visual, auditory and kinesthetic. It will assist both teachers and school counselors to expand their concepts of teaching and learning to include the more "brain-friendly" approach.

Simply put, this means presenting content to students in ways that the brain learns best. We don't have to be neuroscientists to understand how the brain learns naturally. In his book, *Superteaching*, Jensen suggests that we remember how we learned as babies: through multi-sensory experiences, emotion, play, humor, rest and relaxation, fantasy and imagination, a stimulating environment, games, and physical activity.

From 1990 to 1995, I was fortunate to work in the highly successful "Supercamp" program, originally developed by Jensen and Bobbi DePorter. It was in this program that I experienced the power and effectiveness of multisensory learning. It changed my mind forever, and as a result, changed my counseling and teaching methods.

Over the years, I have worked with many students who were considered behavior problems in the classroom. However, I often found that many of these students were adapting to the environment in the only way they knew how. According to Dr. Thomas Gordon, author of *Parent Effectiveness Training*, "Children don't misbehave, they behave to get their needs met." Isn't this true for all of us?

Meeting the Educational Needs of All Students

One learns through the heart, not the eyes or the intellect.

Mark Twain

A counselor once shared the following story with me. The school in which she worked was having a problem with parents and children coming onto the grassy playground area during the weekends. When the school administrator had a fence installed to keep people out, each weekend, a hole would be cut in the fence and, once again, community members could be seen picnicking and playing ball on the grass. When I asked this counselor why she thought the problem was occurring, she confided that the community had no park within walking distance of the school, and that many of the families did not own cars.

Would we say then that these parents were "misbehaving," or would it be safe to say that there was a need for a park in the neighborhood and that the school and community should work together to solve the problem?

Finding solutions often requires us to think in new ways. By identifying the needs, appropriate solutions become visible and possible.

Educators today are faced with the multiple challenges of meeting the needs of very diverse school populations, but when we try to make all students learn in the same way, we create more problems by "trying to fit the square peg into the round hole."

In his book, *How the Brain Learns*, Dr. David Sousa says: "Because today's students are accustomed to quick change and novelty in their environment, many find it difficult to concentrate on the same topic for long periods of time."

When children need to move, they will find ways to do it, such as by fidgeting, talking to their neighbors, or just getting up and walking around. This is often seen as misbehavior in the classroom, and many of these students end up in our counseling centers with discipline referrals.

The lessons in this book are designed to get students moving, thinking, talking and enjoying themselves while learning. I have found that students of all ages, cultures and genders like to learn this wa. That includes my graduate students at the university.

Why Focus on Emotional Intelligence?

Emotion is the chief source of all becoming conscious.

C.G. Jung

Neuroscientist Dr. Candace Pert has done the brain research from which she shows that *molecules of emotion run every system in our body.* What this means for teachers is that we have to understand that students do not leave their emotions at the door of the classroom, and that the emotional state of the student can determine whether he or she will be receptive to learning that day. For example, I start my university classes with sharing. Similar to what a kindergarten teacher does, I want to establish a positive relationship with my students every day.

What it means for school counselors is that we have a responsibility to help students develop the skills of Emotional Intelligence so that they can achieve maximum success in school and in their lives.

And finally, for students, it means that being able to feel their feelings, identify their needs and communicate them to others, puts them in control of their lives.

According to author Daniel Goleman, "At best, IQ contributes about 20 percent to the factors that determine life success, which leaves 80 percent to other forces."

The other forces that Goleman refers to include such things as: self-discipline, empathy, persistence, zest for living, anger management, and the ability to understand one's connection with all people and all things. Goleman goes on to define the three key areas of Emotional Intelligence as: Self-Awareness, Managing Emotions and Relationship Skills, which include Communication and Conflict Resolution.

Children who learn to recognize feelings in others learn to empathize and relate to others. They are able to understand how their behavior affects the people around them and in the larger world. We could say that violence prevention is best done by teaching the skills of Emotional Intelligence.

How to Use This Book

One cannot learn to swim by being sprinkled with water.

Li Mongtao

The lessons in this book are divided into the three broad areas of Emotional Intelligence:

1. Self-Awareness
2. Managing Emotions
3. Relationship Skills.

Each lesson has goals relating to Emotional Intelligence. These goals also relate to competencies identified in the National Standards for School Counseling Programs.

I have cross-referenced the activity goals of the lessons in the book with school counseling program standards that are based on the National Standards for School Counseling Programs. By viewing the standards and competencies in a matrix at the end of the book, school counselors can see, at a glance, what areas of the program standards are being covered by this curriculum.

This curriculum is not intended to cover all areas of the school counseling program standards. The focus will be mainly on the personal and social domains of the standards (the Emotional Intelligences), and they are applicable to both elementary and secondary students.

Presentation

The best discipline is the one no one notices.

Robert E. Lee

The implementation of a curriculum or program can make the difference between simply "going through the motions" or getting real results. Following the steps in this format will prove to be fun for the counselor as well as the students. While there is preparation needed for the lessons, I believe that it will be well worth the effort. I have used these lessons with many different audiences of all ages and have found them to be highly successful.

Their use is limited only by your imagination and creativity. I don't suggest an age range for individual lessons, because I have met youngsters who are wise beyond their years, and I have met adults who lack these critical life skills. This book can be used with students of all ages to empower them to create the life they desire through Emotional Intelligence and a love of learning.

The format has been adapted from the "Supercamp" presentation model, and may also look similar to other lesson plans you have used. However, a key to this presentation style is to keep the learning multisensory, active, positive and fun. Each activity is written with six distinct format components. In order to make the activities as effective as possible, it is important to present each component and to do them in the order listed. Suggestions are provided for questions and information to give to the students, but feel free also to create your own based on the needs, experiences and readiness of your students.

Format

- SET THE STAGE: Build rapport with the students by asking an engaging question or making an interesting quote or comment. This is also a good time to announce the topic or state the goal of the lesson.

- MODEL THE CONCEPT: Role-plays, poems, video clips, stories, jokes, songs or other experiential activities are kinesthetic strategies that can create the "aha" moments of learning. It makes your learner want to know more.

- MINI-LECTURE AND QUESTION: Asking thought-provoking questions allows the learner to interact with the content and give it personal meaning. This is where you can provide the details. But remember the quote, "Be brief, be brilliant, and be seated." This is why I call it the mini-lecture. Keep your focus on the students. If you see attention wandering, ask a question, ask for feedback, or create movement by having students change seats, get a drink of water, stretch or discuss in pairs the information they just received. Be creative!

- PRACTICE: Participants learn best when they can interact with the new concept and demonstrate their proficiency. Strategies such as cooperative learning groups, projects, role-plays, planning and sharing are useful here. This is the time to step aside and let the students take charge of their learning.

- REVIEW: Asking students to review what they have learned helps to integrate the concepts into the learner's belief system. It can be done by large-group sharing, partner sharing, mapping the information, skits, etc.

- CELEBRATE: Acknowledge both the success of a job well done as well as effort, even if it produced less than desirable results. By acknowledging the effort, we encourage students to learn from their mistakes as well as from their successes. Continually notice and acknowledge students when they are "caught" using their new skills!

We must continually strive to find effective ways to teach and reach all students.

If we launch a student into the technological, complex world we live in, without emotional and academic literacy, we invite a nightmare scenario for this person, who could possibly be lost for life.

Michael Dove

Our overcrowded prisons and juvenile detention facilities are prime examples. We cannot continue to punish people for not using skills that they have never been taught. Why should we change what we are doing? If the old paths no longer serve us, then why not take off in a new direction?

I've included this Mind Map™ to illustrate in pictures and words the flow of the format of the lessons. My example is for the first lesson, "The Comfort Zone." This will be helpful to those who appreciate a visual and/or kinesthetic approach to learning new information.

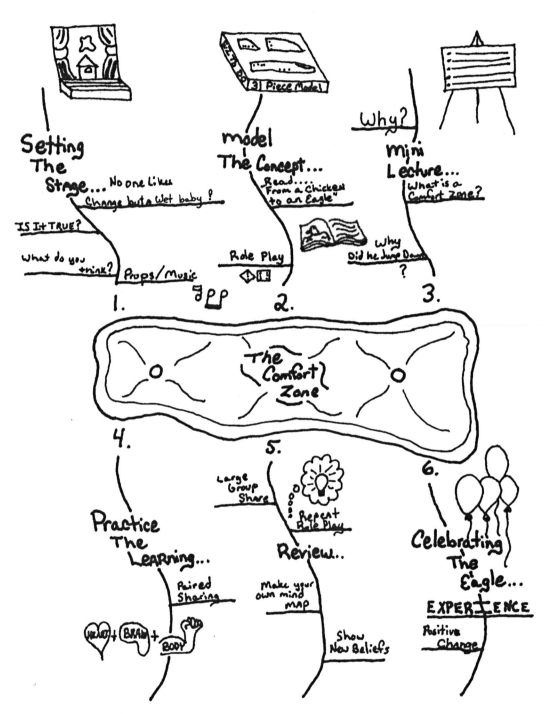

Created by Chris Daly, 2003
Mind Mapping® is a registered trademark of the Buzan Centres, Ltd.

Introduction

Part One

Self-Awareness

We do not grow absolutely, chronologically.
We grow sometimes in one dimension, and not in another, unevenly.
We grow partially.
We are relative.
We are mature in one realm, childish in another.
The past, present and future mingle and pull us backward, forward,
Or fix us in the present.
We are made up of layers, cells, constellations.

Anais Nin

The Comfort Zone

Materials:

The story "The Chicken and the Eagle"
An eagle puppet and a chicken puppet that peeps

Option: Students can also role play without the puppets

Goals:

— To learn to accept change as a natural process to personal growth
— To be able to move beyond fear and take healthy risks
— To be able to detach from old negative programming

Set the Stage:

Say to students, *Do you remember when you first came to _____ school? What did it feel like to make the change from your old school?* Allow the students to share. Next ask, *Have you ever heard the expression, "No one likes change but a wet baby?" What do you think that means?* (Many people fear change, because it is uncomfortable.)

Lead a brief discussion about changes that students have made in their lives. Share a change you have experienced in your life, as well. After the discussion say, *I'd like to read a story to you about personal change.*

Model:

Read the story, "The Chicken and the Eagle," by Jerry Fankhauser. Ask for two student volunteers to role-play the story as you read it aloud. One student can be the eagle and the other the chicken. The student who plays the eagle does as the story describes. The student who plays the chicken should make the chicken peep or make peeping sounds each time chickens are mentioned in the story.

Mini-Lecture and Questions:

1. Why did the eagle think he was a chicken? (He grew up with chickens and all the messages he received about himself were that he was also a chicken. It was all that he knew.)
2. Why did the eagle continually jump back down to be with the chickens even though the naturalist tried to show him how to fly? (He was

afraid. He didn't know that he could fly. The chicken coop felt safe and comfortable to him.)

3. How was he creating his own prison? (His limiting beliefs that he couldn't fly kept him from flying.)
4. What is a comfort zone? (A place that is familiar to us and where we feel safe.)
5. What would have happened to the eagle if he had stayed in his comfort zone? (He would never have discovered who he was really meant to be — an eagle who could fly.)
6. Do people have comfort zones? What happens if they always stay in their comfort zone? (They don't learn and grow to develop their full potential.)
7. Do people sometimes get wrong messages about who they are? Give some examples. (students believing that they can't learn, adults believing that they aren't capable or worthy of success)
8. What are some examples of healthy risk-taking that will expand our comfort zones? (making new friends, taking a class that seems difficult, asking for help, learning a new skill such as playing an instrument, taking on a position of leadership)
9. What happens when we gain new experiences? (We expand our comfort zones. It helps us to develop ourselves.)

Practice:

Have the students get into pairs and share with their partners: A time when I was out of my comfort zone and it helped when I made a change for the better.

Review:

Ask the students, *Who would like to volunteer to share with the class what you shared with your partner?* Allow time for sharing. Conclude by asking, *What have we learned?*

Celebrate:

Acknowledge the students' efforts. Encourage them to continue taking healthy risks to expand their comfort zones. The class could schedule a regular "Eagle Report Time" to share new experiences or projects.

The Chicken and the Eagle

One day a naturalist who was passing a barnyard inquired of the owner why it was that an eagle, the king of all birds, should be confined to live in the barnyard with the chickens.

"Since I have given the eagle chicken feed and trained it to be a chicken, it has never learned to fly," replied the owner. "It behaves as chickens behave, so it is no longer an eagle."

"Still," insisted the naturalist, "it has the heart of an eagle and can surely be taught to fly." After talking it over, the two men agreed to find out whether this was possible. Gently the naturalist took the eagle in his arms and said, "You belong to the sky and not to the earth. Stretch forth your wings and fly.

The eagle, however, was confused; he did not know who he was. Seeing the chickens eating their food, he jumped down to be with them again.

Undismayed, on the following day the naturalist took the eagle up on the roof of the house and urged him again, saying, "You are an eagle. Stretch forth your wings and fly." But the eagle was afraid of his unknown self and afraid of the big world and so he jumped down once more for the chicken food.

On the third day the naturalist rose early and took the eagle out of the barnyard to a high mountain. There he held the king of birds high above him and encouraged him again, saying, "You are an eagle. You belong to the sky as well as the earth. Stretch forth your wings now and fly.)

The eagle looked back towards the barnyard and up to the sky. Still he did not fly. Then the naturalist lifted him straight towards the sun, and it happened that the eagle began to tremble; slowly he stretched his wings. At last, with a triumphant cry he soared in the sky.

It may be that the eagle still remembers the chickens with nostalgia; it may even be that he occasionally revisits the barnyard. But as far as anyone knows, he has never returned to lead the life of a chicken. He was an eagle though he had been kept and tamed as a chicken.

Just like the eagle, people who have learned to think of themselves as something they aren't can re-decide in favor of what they really are.

Reprinted with permission of Jerry Fankhauser.

Café EQ

Materials:

The handouts "What Is Emotional Intelligence or EQ?" and "Café EQ's Special Recipe for a Satisfying Life"
Café music such as the CD "Dinner in Italy" by Avalon Music
Luncheon food or snacks and ice water, paper plates, cups and utensils as necessary to serve and eat the food
Checkered table cloths (optional)
Luncheon invitations (optional)

Goals:

— To introduce the concept of Emotional Intelligence
— To create an environment for joyful learning

Set the Stage:

Invite the students to a special luncheon in the classroom. Provide the invitation, either written or verbal, at least two days prior to the lesson to build excitement. On the day of the lesson, create a café atmosphere with checkered tablecloths, café music, and food.

Model:

Provide simple but healthy food items for the students to eat such as sandwiches, potato salad, vegetables and dip, yogurt and fruit, or have the students bring their school lunches to the classroom and provide cookies or another simple dessert. Let the students enjoy the café atmosphere while they eat.

Mini-Lecture and Questions:

Say to students, *At luncheons, there is usually a guest speaker, and today is no exception. I am your guest speaker and the topic I will speak on is "Emotional Intelligence or EQ."* For your luncheon "speech," provide a brief explanation of Emotional Intelligence using your own words or the following description as a script:

> When we mention the word, "intelligence," most people think of IQ or the ability to learn information and skills, but due to a great deal of research into how the brain works, we now know that emotions, or

feelings contribute to our behavior and to choices that we make that affect our lives. Brain researcher Dr. Daniel Goleman states that IQ contributes at most 20 percent to the factors that determine successful lives. That leaves 80 percent to other factors. Just what are those other factors? That is what we will be learning about today. It is called Emotional Intelligence or EQ.

When you have finished with your "speech," give each student a copy of the handout, "What is EQ?" Lead a discussion by asking the students to use the handout to answer the following questions:

1. What is the difference between IQ and EQ?
2. What are the three key areas of Emotional Intelligence? Why is EQ important? Explain: *According to scientists who study the nervous system, neuroscientists, emotions are carried in molecules in our bloodstream, and they affect every decision we make. Therefore, it is important to be aware of and have control of our emotions so that we can make good choices for ourselves. An example of this would be to feel your anger and be able to express it appropriately.*
3. How is EQ important to learning? (Negative emotions can interfere with learning while positive emotions can enhance learning.)

Practice:

Give the students the handout "Café EQ's Special Recipe for a Satisfying Life." Ask the students to find a partner. Say, *Many cafes are known for their special recipes. Our café EQ features a special "recipe for life."* Ask the partners to read the Café EQ recipe and share with each other why they think these ingredients are important. Ask for volunteers to share with the whole group what they shared with their partners. Have the partners make up their own recipes for EQ success, and display the student recipes throughout the classroom.

Review:

Lead a brief summary discussion by asking the students, *What have we learned about Emotional Intelligence? Do you agree with what we have learned? How can you use this new information in the classroom and at home?* (We can express our feelings, avoid problems by using good communication skills and manage our emotions effectively.)

Celebrate:

Acknowledge the students' efforts. Continue to visit Café EQ with other special recipes for learning and for life success. Enjoy the delicious results!!

Self-Awareness

What Is Emotional Intelligence or EQ?

How Does EQ Differ from IQ?

IQ = Intelligence Quotient
The ability to learn and apply knowledge
> (Relates to our academic skills)

EQ = Emotional Intelligence
The ability to know and manage feelings
> (Relates to our people skills)

What are the three key areas of EQ?

1. Self-Awareness:
   Awareness of our feelings
   Ability to express our feelings

2. Managing Emotions:
   Anger resolution
   Expressing Sadness
   Self-control
   Having a positive attitude (optimism)

3. Relationships:
   Being able to communicate in a caring way
   Knowing how to settle conflicts
   Understanding other people's feelings (empathy)
   Understanding nonverbal communication

Why is EQ important?

It affects our health, our ability to learn, our behavior and our relationships. It also helps us to achieve goals through persistence and optimism.

Source: *EQ in School Counseling* by Carolyn Sheldon

Café EQ's

Special Recipe for a Satisfying Life

1 tablespoon of humor

a generous amount of exercise

1 cup of caring communication

1 ounce of assertiveness

a dozen feelings of all varieties

1 bushel of fun

gobs of healthy food

gallons of fresh, pure water

lots of positive attitude

a dash of empathy

substitute a pinch of heart for a pinch of ego

several goals

1 personal vision for life

sprinkle with conflict resolution skills

and top with swirls of love

Simmer on low heat for a lifetime.

Our Powerful Thoughts

Materials:

None

Goals:

— To experience the mind/body connection
— To learn that a positive mental focus can make us physically stronger
— To understand that a positive focus can help us achieve goals.

Set the Stage:

To introduce this activity, ask the following questions and lead a brief discussion. *Who would like to be healthier, happier and more successful in school? Do you know how to make that happen? Would you like to learn how to do this?*

Model:

In the following guided imagery, elaborate and elicit a response by encouraging the students to see, smell and taste a bright yellow lemon. Ask the students to close their eyes and say, *Imagine a bright yellow lemon. Now imagine yourself cutting the lemon in half … See yourself picking up half of the lemon and squeezing it … Watch the juice ooze out … Now take the lemon half and hold it up to your nose and smell the tangy aroma of the lemon … Put the lemon in your mouth and feel the sour taste spread over your tongue and throughout your entire mouth. Feel your eyes water and your lips pucker as you salivate.*

Allow a few seconds and then say, *Open your eyes. What did you feel or experience during this visualization?* (Most people will experience a sour taste, will salivate and wrinkle their noses.)

Mini-Lecture and Questions:

After the guided imagery, ask the following questions and encourage discussion.

1. Was there a lemon in the room? (There was no lemon and, yet, just the thought of a lemon caused us to wrinkle our noses as we felt increased saliva in our mouths.)
2. Why did that happen? (Our thoughts actually created a physical reaction in our bodies. It caused us to salivate.)
3. What does that tell us about our thoughts? (They are very powerful.)

Self-Awareness

Explain: *Thoughts can also create emotions. Positive thoughts can make us feel happy. Negative thoughts can make us feel depressed. Scientists have also proven that emotions affect our immune system. Our body's immune system helps us to prevent illness by keeping the body strong. If we can create positive emotions, we will have a stronger immune system and be better able to resist illness.*

Follow up with this question:

4. What is an example of positive thinking? (Self-talk such as: "Mrs. Jones gave me a lot of homework. But, if I start now, I'll have it done in time to watch my favorite TV program.)

Practice:

Let the students experience a "muscle-testing" activity that will reinforce the concepts. Muscle testing lets the students see how the body reacts to words.

Ask the students to find a partner and then listen for instructions. Ask one of the partners (partner one) to extend his/her dominant arm. Then ask partner one to think negative thoughts. (Example: I am weak and powerless.) As partner one is thinking negative thoughts, partner two is asked to press on the extended arm of partner one with two fingers, and partner one is to resist the pressure. Tell them to notice how that feels.

Partner one is then asked to take a deep breath and change his/her thoughts to positive ones. (Example: I am strong and powerful.) We may also help by pointing out the student's positive qualities.

Partner two again presses on the arm of partner one with two fingers while partner one again resists. The students should notice that partner one's arm is noticeably stronger when he/she is thinking positive thoughts.

Partners should then exchange places and repeat the process so that each student feels the results.

Review:

Lead a discussion with the whole group. Ask the following questions, *What did you learn from this activity?* (My arm was stronger when I was thinking positive thoughts.) *How will you use this knowledge in your life to create better results?* (I will adopt a more positive attitude so that my thoughts will contribute to a healthier body and mind, which will help me to achieve my goals of academic and social success.)

Tell the students that this lesson is adapted from the book, *You Can't Afford the Luxury of a Negative Thought* by John Rogers and Peter McWilliams.

Ask the students, *What do you think Mr. Rogers and Mr. McWilliams meant by the title of their book?*

Celebrate:

Acknowledge the students' willingness to participate. Encourage them to remember the power of their thoughts.

The Affirmation Clothesline

Materials:

3x5 cards in assorted colors (at least five per student)
A ball of string or ribbon
The song *Hero* by Mariah Carey (on the CD *Music Box*), other upbeat instrumental music

Goals:

— To help students develop the attitude of being a unique and worthy person
— To learn to use affirmations for self-motivation and confidence
— To learn a strategy to reduce stress

Set the Stage:

Lead a brief discussion by asking the students the following questions, *What is self-esteem?* (One answer might be: It is how you generally feel about yourself on a deep level.) *Would you like to learn a strategy to improve your self-esteem?*

Model:

Play the song *Hero* by Mariah Carey, and ask the students to listen carefully to the words.

Mini-Lecture and Questions:

After listening to the song, ask the following questions and encourage discussion:

1. How does this song make you feel about yourself?
2. What do these words from the song mean to you?
   If you look inside your heart, you don't have to be afraid of what you are.
   When you feel like hope is gone, look inside you and be strong.
   See the truth that a hero lies in you.

3. Do you see yourself as your own hero?
4. What kind of messages do you give yourself?

Summarize by explaining: *Affirmations are positive messages that we give ourselves. Affirmations can help motivate us to accomplish goals or to have more self-confidence. Using all of your senses helps make the affirmations more effective. You*

Self-Awareness

do this by saying your affirmations out loud or in your mind, by visualizing them in your mind as pictures of the things you want, and by feeling them "in your heart" as the song tells us.

Saying affirmations in the morning can set your intentions for a positive and productive day. You can also close your eyes and say your affirmations to relieve stress at any time in the day. The more you say, think and feel your affirmations, the more powerful they become.

Practice:

Have the students work in pairs or small groups to brainstorm affirmations. (Play upbeat instrumental music while they work together.)

Give the students a 3-foot length of string and the 3x5 cards, and tell them to fold the cards in half vertically. Have the students write affirmations on both sides of the cards and hang them on the string or ribbon like a clothesline. Suggest that the students hang their affirmation clothesline in a spot where they will look at it every day, such as on the bathroom mirror. They can say or think their affirmations as they brush their teeth or comb their hair.

Review:

Ask the class to review what they have learned about affirmations. Let the students suggest other ways to use the affirmation clotheslines. Examples:

- Hang them up in the classroom or around the school.
- Put affirmations in the school newsletters.
- Start each morning in class with an affirmation.
- Invite a motivational speaker to the class.

Celebrate:

Acknowledge the students' work on this activity and continue to recognize and model positive self-talk.

The Choice Is Yours

Materials:

A graduation cap and gown
Marching music
The handout "Goal setting"

Goals:

— To learn how to set and achieve goals
— To learn the importance of keeping goals in mind when making choices
— To understand how feelings influence choices
— To help teh students take responsibility for their future

Set the Stage:

March into the classroom, with music playing, wearing a graduation cap and gown. Say, *Graduating from college was a goal I set for myself many years ago. It is one of my proudest achievements. How many of you have the goal to go to college? Do you have a plan for reaching that goal?*

Model:

Say to the students, *Reaching my goal was not easy. There were many obstacles I had to overcome.* (Share a few of your obstacles.) *Everyone has an interesting story, so don't hesitate to share.* Only a few minutes are needed to get the students interested.

Mini-Lecture and Questions:

Give each student a copy of the handout "Goal setting." Ask the following questions and lead a brief discussion.

1. What does the picture illustrate? (Goals can be easier to reach when we break them down into smaller steps.)
2. How do poor choices keep us from reaching our goals? (Inappropriate behavior or poor choices can take us in a direction away from our goals.)
3. What are some examples of poor choices? (using drugs or alcohol, skipping school, not doing homework)

Self-Awareness

4. How might we stay on track to reach our goals? (Keep your goals in mind when making choices. Post your goals where you can look at them every day.)
5. What might be some barriers you will face? (examples: peer pressure, stress, family problems, academic problems)
6. What are some strategies you might use to overcome these barriers? (Talk to someone you trust, learn to set boundaries with friends, join a counseling group, exercise to reduce stress, maintain a good relationship with parents and family, get academic help from teachers or a tutor.)

Advise the students that goals can be short-term, as in a goal for the day. (Examples: Secondary level student: I will be on time to all of my classes today. Elementary level: I will be on time for school today.) Goals can also be long-term as in a goal for the year. (Example: Secondary level student: I will make the honor roll each quarter. Elementary level: I will pass the fourth grade with all A's and B's.)

Practice:

Let the students work individually to write a goal for tomorrow. Then have them write a goal for the week, the month and the year. Ask for volunteers to share their goals with the group.

Review:

Ask, *What did you learn about setting and attaining goals?*

Review the following concepts with the students and elicit discussion:

- Goals are more easily attainable when they are broken down into small steps.
- Goals can help us to be more organized as we identify and focus on our priorities.
- Goals can keep us on track.

With persistence, we can create our futures by setting and reaching goals.

Celebrate:

Congratulate the students for taking responsibility for creating their futures by setting goals. Let them share and be recognized for goals that are attained.

Goal Setting

Sometimes a goal like "going to college" looks overwhelming, but by developing a love of learning, working hard, using self-discipline, and being persistent, you can earn the good grades needed to go to college.

Short-term goals that can help you reach the long-term goal of college might look like this:

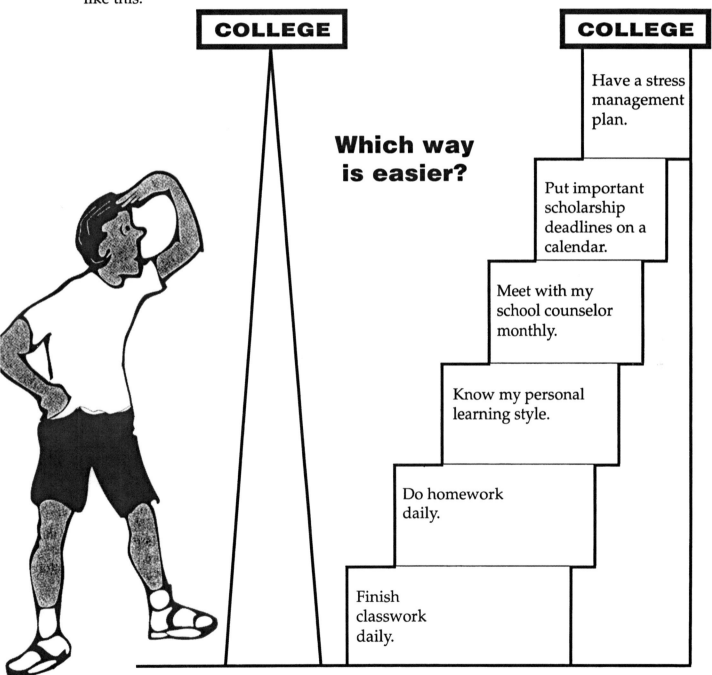

I Am Somebody

Materials:

A copy of the quote "I Am Somebody" for each student. (I suggest duplicating the quote on colorful paper.)

Goals:

— To develop a positive attitude toward self as a unique and worthy person
— To identify personal strengths and assets

Set the Stage:

Lead a brief discussion by asking these questions, *Have you ever had a problem that you thought you couldn't solve* (examples: a problem with a teacher, with a parent or with a friend)? *Did you look for someone else to solve the problem? What was the result?*

Model:

Give each student a copy of the handout. Say, *Let's read this quote and think about what it means.* Read it to the class and ask, *What do you think this quote means?* (Often, we don't recognize the gifts and talents we have, or we may lack confidence in our own abilities. We look to other people to solve our problems for us.)

Mini-Lecture and Questions:

Say, *Many people think of strengths as characteristics that others can see and admire. However, there are many qualities, such as our Emotional Intelligence, that give us an inner strength, and when we learn to trust this inner strength, we often find that we have the answers we need and can solve our own problems.*

Encourage the students to share by asking, *What is a personal strength or talent that you have but don't often recognize or take the time to think about?* To get the discussion going share a strength or talent you possess. (Examples: a caring attitude, ability to cook, loyalty, honesty, the ability to think through a problem, etc.)

Practice:

Ask each of the students to create a project to show his or her positive qualities and personal strengths that others may not see. Explain that the project

Self-Awareness

can be in any form that appeals to him or her. Some examples might be: write a story, compose a song, give a talk to the class on a topic that is important to you, draw a picture, write a poem, or pantomime or act out a scene to teach something to the class.

Review:

Have a large group share. Ask the students, *What have you learned or remembered about yourself by doing your individual project?*

Celebrate:

Acknowledge the students' willingness to get out of their comfort zones by sharing something about themselves. Display the individual projects.

I Am Somebody

I kept looking for somebody
to solve the problem,
and then I realized,
I am somebody.

Anonymous

Be Careful Your Thoughts

Materials:

Poster boards and colorful pens

Goals:

— To understand the relationship between thoughts, feelings and actions
— To learn to take responsibility for our lives
— To understand that thoughts can create our reality

Set the Stage:

Ask the students the following questions and lead a brief discussion, *Who do you feel is in control of your life?* (Students may answer "parents," "teachers," etc.) *Would you like to have more control of your life? How can you make that happen?*

Model:

Write the following quote where students can easily see it.

> *Be careful your thoughts, they become actions.*
> *Be careful your actions, they become habits.*
> *Be careful your habits, they become your character.*
> *Be careful your character, it becomes your destiny.*

> William Makepeace Thackeray

Ask the students to read the quote and think about what it means.

Mini-Lecture and Questions:

Ask the following questions and lead a brief discussion.

1. What do you think William Thackeray meant by this quote?
2. Do you agree with him? Why?
3. What are some ways in which this applies to your life?

Summarize by explaining, *If I think negative thoughts about someone, the chances are that I may begin to treat the person in a negative way. My thoughts will affect my behavior, and if a behavior gets repeated often, it can become a habit. By being more conscious of my thoughts, I can control my actions, habits and my character. By keeping positive thoughts that are focused on my goals, I can create my destiny by achieving my goals.*

Practice:

Let the students make colorful posters with this quote to display at home and at school. Let it be a continual reminder that they are in control of their lives. Have the students follow up on this activity by finding other quotes that are meaningful to them. Let them share and discuss the meanings with the class.

Review:

Ask students, *How has the Thackeray quote affected your outlook on life?*

Celebrate:

Acknowledge the students' efforts by letting them choose a quote to begin each day. Continually acknowledge improved student behavior in class.

Life Is a Balancing Act

Materials:

Handout "Life is a Balancing Act."

Goals:

— To demonstrate the need to balance academic, career and personal areas of life

— To develop an awareness of abilities, skills and interests in these areas

Set the Stage:

Ask the students the following questions and lead a brief discussion, *How many of you have ever seen a tightrope act at the circus? What is the most important element of the act?* (Balance.) *What is balance?* (The dictionary defines balance as to be equal in weight or value; harmony or a sense of well-being.) *How is balance an important element in your life?* (I'm not balancing on a tightrope, but if I play all the time and don't do homework, I won't get good grades, and if I work all the time and I don't take time to play, I will be stressed out.)

Model:

Ask the class to stand. When all the students are standing, say, *Let's see how long we can stand on one leg without touching anything.* (The students will probably only be able to stand a few minutes before falling over.)

Say, *How long do you think you can "stay on your feet" in life without balancing the key areas of your life?*

Mini-Lecture and Questions:

Ask the following questions and lead a brief discussion,

1. What do you think are three key areas in your life that need to be kept in balance? (academics or school, personal and social or home life, and future or career plans)

2. What are some important skills and abilities to have in each of these areas?

Practice:

Give each student a copy of the handout "Life is a Balancing Act."

Self-Awareness

Ask the students to choose a partner and move to a place in the room where they can comfortably talk.

Say, *Using the handout, work as a team to add your own strategies to the lists.*

Review:

Lead a large group discussion by asking these questions, *What have you learned from this lesson? What kind of help do you need to balance these three areas?*

Celebrate:

Agree to help students in whatever way you can to get their "balancing" act together.

Life Is a Balancing Act

My Academic Life

1. Know how to study
2. Know my preferred learning style

3. _____
4. _____
5. _____
6. _____
7. _____
8. _____

My Personal and Social Life

1. Get enough sleep
2. Eat a nutritious diet; avoid junk food
3. Have good communication skills

4. _____
5. _____
6. _____
7. _____
8. _____

My Career Plans

1. Set goals for myself
2. Make decisions that keep me on track with my goals.

3. _____
4. _____
5. _____
6. _____
7. _____
8. _____

Part Two

Managing Emotions

It is better to light a
Candle than to curse
The Darkness.

Ancient Chinese Proverb

The Magic Doll

Introduction:

The idea for the Magic Doll came from my Aunt Annette. She has a doll that she uses to tell heartwarming stories to all of my cousins. She imparts wisdom and our cultural customs through her stories, and the joy of these stories continues with each generation of grandchildren. This lesson is dedicated to my Aunt Annette.

Materials:

A doll or several dolls of varying ethnicities
Art paper and crayons, markers or paints

Goals:

— To learn to adjust to changing family roles such as in divorce
— To acknowledge that all feelings are important
— To understand that positive self-talk can help us cope with our feelings

Set the Stage:

Ask the following questions and lead a brief discussion:

— *What is divorce?* (When two married people decide to end their marriage.)
— *Why do people get divorced?* (One answer might be that they cannot get along with one another and they cannot settle their differences.)
— *Is divorce ever the children's' fault?* (No, the children don't cause parents to get divorced. That is the parents' decision.)
— *Do all cultures have divorce?* (No, some cultures do not recognize divorce.)

Model:

Say to the students, *Would you like to hear a story about one young girl's experience?* Read the story "The Magic Doll." To enhance the experience, bring a doll to "tell" the story or simply display several dolls on a table.

Mini-Lecture and Questions:

When the story is finished, ask the students the following questions:

1. Why was the little girl sad, even though she had fun at her birthday party?
2. Is it okay to be sad? (Yes, all feelings are important.)
3. What is self-talk? (It is our inner voice or thoughts.)
4. Could the magic doll have been the girl's own thoughts or self-talk?
5. How did her inner voice help her? (By letting her know that she didn't cause her parents' divorce and that both of her parents still loved her.)
6. Who else can we talk to about our feelings? (parents, teachers, school counselors, friends)
7. Can we still be happy after major changes in our families such as divorce, the birth of a new baby, moving to a new city or changing schools? (Yes, even though those events are life changing and sometimes stressful, we can cope with them by recognizing how we feel and talking about our feelings with someone else or making ourselves feel better with our own self talk.)

Practice:

Give each student art paper and drawing materials. Ask them to make a picture of a "Magic Creature." Explain that a creature can be anything they want such as a doll, a robot, a make-believe animal or talking tree. Encourage the students to be creative. When they are finished, let each student share his or her picture with the class and describe the Magic Creature.

Teachers or counselors can then create age-appropriate activities to follow up with the "Magic Creatures" such as creative writing, storytelling or role playing. In a small counseling group, the counselor could use the activity to say: "If the creature could talk to us, what would it say?"

Review:

Discuss with the large group:

— *What did we learn from our activity today?* (We have learned that it is important to talk about our feelings and that all feelings are important.)
— *How can acknowledging and talking about our feelings help us live happier lives?*

Celebrate:

Acknowledge the students' efforts and display the "Magic Creature" pictures in the classroom.

Managing Emotions

The Magic Doll

There once was a young mother who had a beautiful little girl. She loved her daughter very much and wanted to be the best mother she could be. Just before her daughter's fifth birthday, she decided that she wanted to have a birthday party for her daughter and give her a very special gift.

The young mother didn't have a lot of money to spend and so she looked and looked for just the right gift that she could afford. Finally, she went into a toy store, where she spotted a small doll high up on a shelf. The doll was dusty, as if she had been there for a long time, and so the shopkeeper sold the doll to the mother at a very good price.

On the day of the party, all of the little girl's friends came to her house. They had a wonderful party, and she received many gifts. The last present she was given was the present from her mother. When she opened the box, she saw the beautiful little doll. It was the most beautiful doll she had ever seen, and she instantly loved her.

That evening as the little girl was getting ready to go to bed, she thought about her party and wished she had been able to share it with her father, who lived in another city. She started to cry. Just then, she heard a soft voice say, "Didn't we have a wonderful party?"

The little girl looked around to see who was talking. She said out loud, "Who said that?"

"I did," said the doll.

"But dolls don't talk," said the little girl with an astonished look on her face.

"Well, I do because I'm a magic doll. I know that you miss your father, and I wanted to let you know that even though he isn't here, he loves you as your mother does. Your parents decided not to live together any more. But that had nothing to do with their love for you. They both love you very much."

Upon hearing that and knowing it was the truth, the little girl felt much better, and then fell fast asleep with her magic doll in her arms.

Of course, on the next day, the little girl told her mother about the magic doll. Her mother laughed and acted as if she believed her daughter, even though she had her doubts.

The little girl had many wonderful days after that with her magic doll. She grew into her teens, graduated from high school and left home to go to college.

As she grew up, she spent less and less time with her doll, until finally, the doll sat on the shelf and was forgotten.

One day the little girl, all grown up now, and married, had a little girl of her own. On her little girl's fifth birthday, she wanted to give her daughter something very special, and she remembered the doll from her childhood. She took it off the shelf where it had sat forgotten for many years, dusted it off, and wrapped it in pretty paper.

Her daughter was so excited when she saw the doll. She hugged the doll and played all day with the doll and held it in her arms when she went to bed. The next morning the little girl said to her mother, "Mommy, my doll talked to me last night. She's a magic doll."

"That's not possible," said the mother. "Dolls don't ..." She stopped. Instantly, she remembered that this was a magic doll; one who comforted her on many nights when she had missed her father. Then the mother smiled a big smile and said, "Of course, she is. And, she is a very smart doll too. Because of her, I always knew that I was loved."

Perseverance Pays Off

Introduction:

This activity comes from a personal experience of mine. I decided to make real whipping cream one day. As I began to use the electric mixer, I became more and more frustrated when the whipping cream was still a runny liquid. Just as I was about to give up, I had a bowl of fluffy, white whipping cream. I learned the important lesson to persevere rather than give up. I decided to try the lesson with a class of graduate school counseling students, and they loved it! I hope you will, too.

Materials:

A bowl of strawberries large enough for the whole class
Five or six cartons of either light or heavy whipping cream (Light cream takes even longer to whip.)
Mixing bowls, spoons, forks, paper plates, napkins, five or six hand mixers
Upbeat music, and the home video "Rudy" (available at most video rental stores)

Goal:

— To understand the value of perseverance in reaching a goal

Set the Stage:

Ask, *Who has ever been frustrated and given up when trying to reach a goal? What is perseverance?* (Sticking with something until it is finished, refusing to give up.) *How could perseverance have helped you in your situation?*

Model:

Divide the class into five or six groups. Give each group a hand mixer (you may choose to use portable electric mixers), a bowl, and a carton of whipping cream. Have a competition between the groups to see which group can make whipped cream first. (Use heavy cream with hand mixers and light cream with electric mixers.) The students in each group should take turns whipping the cream.

The competition will create the urgency to get the cream whipped quickly and will help to build some frustration. Observe who wants to give up. Play upbeat music while the teams are whipping the cream. Declare a winner!

Mini-Lecture and Questions:

After the contest is over, ask the following questions:

1. What created the frustration during the activity? (the competition, the length of time it took the cream to stiffen, the team not working together)
2. Did you ever think you weren't going to be successful?
3. How did that feel?
4. Who felt like giving up? What made you continue?
5. How does perseverance pay off? (In academics, careers and in our personal lives, we have to stick with our challenges to overcome them.)

Explain that perseverance is one of the Emotional Intelligence or EQ skills.

6. How might perseverance be just as important or even more important than IQ in reaching goals? (No matter what your skills are, if you give up because of challenges, the goal won't be reached.)

Practice:

Show the video "Rudy." This can be done either on the same day or the next. Discuss this remarkable, true story by asking, *How did Rudy achieve his goal of playing football for Notre Dame University?* Ask the students to share examples of times when they persevered, and it paid off in a positive way.

Review:

Ask, *What have you learned about perseverance? How will you use this concept in reaching future goals?*

Celebrate:

Let everyone eat the strawberries and whipped cream that you have brought to class! The delight of their taste buds will make this a memorable lesson.

I Can Laugh at Me!

Materials:

Handout "The Cookie Thief"
Enough cookies for the class

Goals:

— To learn that one can be wrong even while feeling right
— To learn the importance of expressing our true feelings
— To learn that it is okay to make mistakes

Set the Stage:

Ask the following questions and lead a brief discussion:

— *Have you ever felt absolutely sure that you were right about something, and then found out that you were mistaken? How did you feel?*
— *Could you laugh at yourself?*

Model:

Say, *Listen while I read a poem that will remind us to laugh at our mistakes rather than be angry or embarrassed.*

Give each student a copy of the handout "The Cookie Thief." Read the poem with inflection and drama.

Mini-Lecture and Questions:

After you have read the poem, ask the following questions and lead a brief discussion.

1. What mistake did the lady in the poem make? (She thought that the man was taking her cookies when she was actually eating his cookies.)
2. What would you have done if you thought someone was eating your cookies?
3. What could the lady have said to the man? ("Excuse, me but these are my cookies. Would you like one?")
4. What did the lady choose to do instead? (She hid her true feelings.)
5. Is it okay to make mistakes? (Yes, we all make mistakes.)

Managing Emotions

Practice:

Divide the students into groups of three or four. Ask the students to share a time when they thought they were right but they found out later that they were actually wrong. Provide an example of your own. (Example: "One time I was angry that another woman took a parking space that I was about to enter. A few moments later, I realized that I was traveling the wrong way on the street.")

After all the small groups have shared, ask for volunteers to share their stories with the large group.

Review:

Ask, *What did we learn from this poem?*

Celebrate:

Enjoy the cookies!!

THE COOKIE THIEF

A woman was waiting at an airport one night
with several long hours before her flight.
She hunted for a book in the airport shop,
bought a bag of cookies and found a place to drop.

She was engrossed in her book but happened to see
that the man beside her, as bold as could be,
grabbed a cookie or two from the bag between
which she tried to ignore to avoid a scene.

She munched cookies and watched the clock
as the gutsy cookie thief diminished her stock.
She was getting more irritated as the minutes ticked by
thinking, "If I wasn't so nice, I'd blacken his eye."

When only one was left, she wondered what he'd do.
With a smile on his face and a nervous laugh,
he took the last cookie and broke it in half.

He offered her half as he ate the other,
She snatched it from him and thought,
"Oh brother!"

This guy has some nerve and he's also rude.
Why, he didn't even show any gratitude.
She had never known when she had been so galled,
and sighed with relief when her flight was called.

She gathered her belongings and headed to the gate,
refusing to look back at that thieving ingrate.

She boarded the plane and sank in her seat, then
sought her book, which was almost complete.
As she reached in her baggage, she gasped with surprise.
There was her bag of cookies in front of her eyes.

If mine are here, she moaned with despair,
then the others were his and he tried to share.
Too late to apologize, she realized with grief,
that she was the rude one, the ingrate, and the thief.

Valerie Cox

Anger: Use It and Lose It!

Materials:

Two or three newspaper articles about violent behavior
The handout, "What's Beneath The Anger?" (paper puppets)
Popsicle sticks and glue

Optional: Stuffed animal puppets (enough for each student)

Goals:

— To learn that, like all emotions, anger has a purpose
— To learn that fear and sadness are often root causes of anger
— To understand that "out of control" anger can lead to violence
— To learn how to express anger appropriately in order to resolve it

Set the Stage:

Bring in two or three stories from the local newspaper that deal with angry behavior. Pick articles with clear-cut conflict situations. Read the articles and ask the students what they think contributed to the violence. Lead a brief discussion.

Model:

Give each student a copy of the handout "What's Beneath The Anger." Have them cut out the dog and two cat paper puppets and glue each puppet to a stick. (Optional: Use real puppets for the role-play.)

Have the students choose a partner, and role-play with each other. One to role-play with the cat puppets and the other with the dog puppet.

Lead the students through the role-play by asking, *How many of you have a cat? What is your cat like when he is happy and contented?*

Ask the students with the cat puppets to show with their docile cat puppet how a cat would be acting if it was feeling happy. (Encourage the students to use sounds and actions as they role-play the cat.)

Now ask, *Have you ever seen a cat change its behavior very quickly? What would happen if the dog puppet came bouncing into the room up to the cat?*

The student with the dog puppet is to charge toward the cat again using sounds and actions. Now the students show the aggressive cat puppet and vividly demonstrate how the cat would change its behavior and react angrily towards the dog.

Mini-Lecture and Questions:

Have the students set the puppets aside, and begin the discussion. Ask the students the following questions and lead a brief discussion.

1. Why did the cat become aggressive? (The dog startled him.)
2. Although the cat became angry and aggressive, what was he feeling beneath the anger? (He was afraid of the dog.)
3. Do you think that fear might also cause people to become angry? (Yes, fear is often an emotion beneath anger.)
4. How does anger lead to aggressive or violent behavior? (When people don't know how to express their anger appropriately, they may choose to express their anger in an aggressive or violent manner. Uncontrollable anger is also called rage.)

Explain to the students that anger is a signal that something is wrong. We may be angry because of fear, but we may also get angry because we are sad about something. For this reason, anger is a useful emotion. Here are some steps that we can take to resolve the anger. This means we should get help for the underlying problem rather than to just "control" the angry feelings.

Steps for resolving anger:

- Stop and take a deep breath.
- Ask, "What am I feeling right now?"
- "Why am I angry?"
- "What do I need?"
- Get what I need by helping myself or asking someone else to help me.

5. How can you use this knowledge to help people who are angry? (We might ask them what is bothering them and encourage them to talk about their feelings or go to an adult for help.)

Practice:

Lead a discussion with the class. Ask, *What are some appropriate ways to express anger without hurting ourselves or anyone else?*

List all of the suggestions on the board. The following are some examples.

- Talk to a counselor, teacher, parent or friend.
- Write down the angry thoughts.
- Write down what I need.
- Express my feelings through art.
- Exercise.
- Drink water to reduce my stress.
- Talk directly to the person I am angry with.

Review:

Ask the students, *Why is it important to be aware of our anger and to know how to express it appropriately?* (Anger can interfere with learning, and with relationships. If left unresolved, anger can lead to rage and violent behavior. Anger resolution is another EQ skill, which can help us to have more confidence in ourselves and higher self-esteem.)

Celebrate:

Encourage the students to acknowledge each other for their efforts to understand their anger responses. Remind them that they are contributing to a safer school environment by being a better classmate and a more responsible citizen.

What's Beneath the Anger?

Inner and Outer Power

Materials:

The handout "The Wind and The Sun"
A jacket or cloak for the role play
A sun drawn on yellow paper
The face of the wind drawn on blue paper

Goals:

— To distinguish between mental and physical strength
— To learn that influential power is more effective than coercive power
— To learn to solve conflicts peacefully

Set the Stage:

Ask the students, *Has anyone ever tried to make you do something you didn't want to do? How did you feel about it? Did you do what they asked?*

Tell the students that you are going to read to them an Aesop fable about power entitled "The Wind and the Sun."

Next ask, *Do you know who Aesop was?* (He was a Greek slave who had to disguise his messages in stories. He often used animals as the characters.) *What is a fable?* (a fictional story with a hidden message or lesson)

Model:

Give each student a copy of the handout "The Wind and The Sun." Ask for three volunteers to role-play the characters in the story as you read it.

Mini-Lecture and Questions:

After reading the story, ask the following questions:

1. What is the moral or lesson in this fable? (Kindness and gentle persuasion are stronger than brute force.)
2. What kind of power did the wind have? (outer or physical power)
3. What kind of power did the sun have? (inner or influential power)
4. Why did the sun win the contest? (The wind was using brute force to try to rip the cloak off the man. The sun was able to influence the traveler so that the traveler changed his own mind and removed the cloak himself.)

5. Do you agree or disagree with the lesson that Aesop was teaching? Why?

Practice:

Put the following questions on the board.

1. How do some students use physical or coercive power? (gangs, bullying)
2. Why do people use this kind of power? (It may be that they want to control others, because they feel out of control themselves.)
3. How do you feel when someone uses this kind of power over you?
4. How can we use our inner brain power to influence and help others who feel out of control? (Don't get into verbal power struggles with them, walk away, stay positive, be a good listener, offer to help them talk to a counselor, peer counselor or teacher.)

Divide the students into groups of three or four and ask them to discuss the answers to the questions among themselves. Suggest that one person record the answers. (Circulate and assist the students as needed.) Let each group give a summary of their answers to the total class.

Review:

Review by asking these final questions to the large group. *What kind of power do you use when you find yourself in a conflict? Has the story changed your mind about power? How can you use this information in your life?* (in school, on a job, in personal relationships)

Celebrate:

Encourage the students to assume leadership opportunities at school, in the community or at home, where they can use their inner brain power to initiate positive action.

As a follow-up activity, invite student leaders such as peer mediators to come into the class to talk about resolving conflicts peacefully by using brain power.

Suggest that the students read books on the lives of Dr. Martin Luther King, Mahatma Gandhi and Peace Pilgrim. (If these are young children, the teacher or counselor can bring in these biographies and share them with the students.)

The Wind and the Sun

The North Wind and the Sun were arguing over which was the most powerful. They decided on a contest to prove which was the stronger. Just then a traveler was coming down the road. "I know how we can prove it," said the Sun. "Let's agree that he who can make the traveler take off his cloak is the stronger."

The North Wind went first and tried to show his power by blowing with all his might to rip the cloak from the man's shoulders. But the stronger his blasts, the closer the traveler wrapped the cloak around him. At last, the North Wind gave up. "Go ahead and try," he said to the Sun.

The Sun came out from behind the clouds and shone his light and warmth. The traveler began to get hot from the warm rays and decided to take off his cloak.

The moral of the story is that persuasion or influential power is stronger than force.

Teapot Talks

Materials:

The handout "Take a Teapot Talk"

Goals:

— To learn how to identify and express feelings
— To be able to recognize the feelings of others
— To understand that letting it all out explosively is not helpful
— To be able to recognize nonverbal communication

Set the Stage:

Ask the students, *Have you ever been angry about something and kept it inside until you felt like you'd burst from the pressure?*

Tell the students that they will be looking at someone who is doing just that.

Model:

Ask two students to role-play for the entire class the following scene. Have one student stand with his/her arms tightly crossed, nose in the air and a scowl on his/her face. The second student then asks, *Is anything wrong?* The response is, *No, nothing's wrong. I'm fine.*

The second student asks, *Are you sure?*

First student answers, *Yes, I'm positive, nothing's wrong.*

End the role-play and thank the volunteers.

Mini-Lecture and Questions:

After the roleplay, ask the following questions and lead a brief discussion.

1. Does this student look like nothing is wrong? (Point to student one.)
2. What body language tells you that this person is really angry and not sharing his or her true feelings? (Tightly crossed arms, clenching the teeth, and scowling are ways to keep feelings locked in the body.)
3. Why is it unhealthy to hold in feelings that should be expressed? (When our brain is consumed with angry feelings, it can't do its best thinking, and when any of the other organs in our body get stressed, they can't work as well either.)

Compare holding in the angry feelings to the steam in a teapot.

Managing Emotions

4. What would happen to the teapot if there was no way for the steam to escape gradually? (It would burst or burn up.)
5. What happens if a person bursts open with feelings that have been locked in or stored up for a long time? (They may say or do something violent or unkind.)
6. Would you like to learn about a better way to express feelings?

Practice:

Have the students get into groups of four or five for a "Teapot Talk" or small group discussion. If possible, have peer counselors or college interns help with the facilitation of each group. If you choose, this can be done as a whole group activity.

Hand out "Take a Teapot Talk" to each student. Explain that there are rules to a Teapot Talk. Review the rules listed on the handout. "One person speaks at a time, everyone listens respectfully to the person speaking, what is said in the group is kept confidential by all group members, and you can remain silent if you wish." Make sure all the students understand and agree to follow the rules.

Write the next sample questions on the board and ask the students to share with one another in a "teapot" talk discussion.

What kinds of things make you angry?
How do you handle your anger?
How do you handle disappointment?
Why is it important to express feelings instead of keeping them inside?

Review:

Limit the small group discussion to about half an hour the first time, and then ask the students to share how they felt about the experience. Hold up the handout and explain, *Just as in a real teapot, a Teapot Talk lets you get the steam out, keeps you from blowing your top, helps you feel better, and lets you figure things out.*

Celebrate:

Acknowledge the students' willingness to try something new.

Teachers and school counselors can work together to identify the students who could benefit from group counseling. Teachers could also initiate classroom meetings for problem solving to continue modeling the expression of feelings through discussion.

Managing Emotions

Take a Teapot Talk

Rules for an Effective Teapot Talk

1. One person speaks at a time.

2. Everyone listens respectfully to the person speaking.

3. What is said in the group is kept confidential by all group members.

4. You can remain silent if you wish.

Music Sets the Mood

Materials:

A CD and cassette tape player
A variety of music CDs and tapes

Goals:

— To understand the effect of music on the brain
— To learn to use music as a study tool
— To learn to use music to reduce stress

Set the Stage:

Two days prior to the lesson, assign each students the task of bringing his or her favorite song to class. Do not censor the music initially. This is one way of getting to know the interests of your students.

Let each student tell the name of his or her favorite song and why he or she likes it, but don't play the music at this time.

Then ask the students to put their music away as they listen to a selection of songs that you have chosen to illustrate the power of music.

Model:

Tell the students that you are going to play a series of songs and they are just to listen. (You may want to record a tape earlier with excerpts from the following types of music in the order shown: First, heavy metal; second, rhythm and blues; third, piano music with nature sounds; fourth, new age such as Enya; and finally, baroque music such as Mozart.

Play about two minutes of the selection before changing to the next type of music. Ask the students to try to feel the change in their moods as the music changes from the initial heavy metal to, finally, baroque. Allow no comments until all of the selections have played.

Mini-Lecture and Questions:

After the students have listened to the selection of songs, ask them the following questions, lead a brief discussion and present the new information.

1. *How did you feel as the music changed?* (Some students will insist that the heavy metal music is relaxing to them. You don't need to disagree.)

Explain that this activity is merely to expose them to different kinds of music and to let them feel the music's effect. There is research to show that baroque music tends to slow the heartbeat and relax the brain. Fast paced, heavy metal music will tend to do the opposite.

2. *Which music would seem to be better for studying?*
3. *What kind of music is good to play if you are feeling stressed and would like to relax?* (Everyone is different, and what is relaxing to one may not be relaxing to another. However, it is important to know that music does affect the brain and can be either useful or harmful depending on your choices.)

Practice:

After explaining to the students that songs that contain lyrics that glorify violence, suicide, sex, racism or other highly negative subjects will not be able to be played, allow the students to play the songs that they have brought with them to class.

Explain to the students that they have felt the effects of different kinds of music and ask them in what ways they think that negative lyrics can have a detrimental effect on us mentally and physically? (Yes, as we experienced in the activity "Our Powerful Thoughts," our bodies had a physical reaction to the lemon by just thinking about it. Musical lyrics put thoughts in our minds and can therefore affect our brains in positive or negative ways. It is better for our brains to not listen to negative lyrics.)

Review:

Review by asking the students, *What have we learned from this lesson?* (Answers will vary. It is important for the teacher or counselor to let the students draw their own conclusions.) *Will you make any changes based on what you learned today? What will these changes be?*

Celebrate:

Celebrate by making music an integral part of learning in the classroom. Allow appropriate music to be played in the classroom at appropriate times. Let the students have input on the selection of music.

It's True: You Are What You Eat!

Introduction:

I am including this lesson, because of what I have observed students eating for lunch in the schools. For many students, lunch consists of soda pop, a bag of potato chips, and cookies. I have also asked students if they drink water from the drinking fountains at school, and the answer was a resounding, "No." I believe that the combination of poor nutrition and a lack of water are contributing factors to the larger numbers of discipline referrals that school counselors receive in the afternoon hours. If schools cannot remove "junk" foods from their cafeterias, then we must educate students about healthy eating, so that they can make better choices for themselves.

Materials:

The handout "Water Facts"

Goals:

— To understand that good nutrition supports our physical and mental health as well as our ability to learn
— To learn the importance of water and adequate hydration

Set the Stage:

Ask the students, *How many of you feel that you eat a healthy lunch?*

Next, ask them what foods they ate for lunch that day or the day before, and make a list on the board of the foods that were eaten.

Ask, *How many of you drink seven to eight glasses of water a day?*

Explain that this activity is about how to use nutrition to feel better and get better grades.

Model:

Ask for a volunteer to demonstrate the effect of certain foods on the body. (You will need a small piece of white bread and three almonds.)

Ask the volunteer to put the white bread in his/her mouth and hold it there without chewing it or swallowing. Now, do the muscle-testing exercise that was done in the lesson, "Our Powerful Thoughts." Have the student extend his/her dominant arm. While the bread is still in his/her mouth, press down on the arm and ask the volunteer to resist the pressure. Notice that the arm is weak. Then have the volunteer take the bread out of his or her mouth and put it into a napkin.

Next give the volunteer three almonds and let him/her chew them. Repeat the muscle test. Press down on the same arm.

The students will be able to see the difference in the two experiments. The student will be visibly stronger when eating the almonds. Point out that the bread consists mainly of carbohydrates while the almonds are primarily protein and healthy fats. A slice of a hard boiled egg can also be substituted for the almonds, and the results will be the same.

Ask, *What does this demonstration verify for us?* (The instant that we put something into our mouths, it begins to metabolize and become part of us. We, indeed, are what we eat.)

Tell the students that this exercise also has implications for the use of drugs and alcohol. It shows us the immediate effect of substances on the brain and body, and in actuality, how we behave and who we are.

Mini-Lecture and Questions:

Ask the students the following questions and lead a brief discussion.

1. *What did you learn from the exercise we just did?*
2. *How can you apply this information in your life?* (One suggestion is to read the labels of foods they eat so that they know the percentages of carbohydrates and proteins in the food.)
3. *What about water? Do you know its benefits?*

Give each of the students the handout "Water Facts," and explain that they are going to learn some important facts about water.

Practice:

Let the students sit with a partner to read and discuss "Water Facts." They are to answer the question, *What do these facts mean to me?*

As a follow-up to this lesson, ask the students to begin keeping a log of the foods they eat and the amount of water they drink for the next two days. Partners can work together to help one another complete the assignment.

At the end of the two days, the students should report their results to the class.

After completing this part of the assignment, suggest that, for the next week, the students drink six to eight glasses of water daily and eliminate "junk foods" from their diets. (Junk foods are generally considered to be foods high in fat, and carbohydrates with a low nutrient value.)

At the end of the week, let the students compare their findings. Notice if there is an increase in energy, a greater ability to focus in the classroom, and an improved feeling of well being.

Review:

Have a large group discussion on the benefits of proper nutrition and water intake. (Don't insist that the students change their habits immediately. By exposing them to new information, you have equipped them with the ability to think about and make better choices for themselves.)

Celebrate:

Acknowledge the students' efforts to make better choices for themselves.

The muscle testing activity was contributed by Dr. Brett Mosher of The Mosher Optimal Health Center in Poway, CA.

Water Facts

The average adult body is 55 to 75% water.

Everyday your body must replace 2 quarts of water.

Aside from aiding in digestion and absorption of food, water regulates body temperature, carries nutrients and oxygen to cells, and removes toxins and other wastes.

Brain tissue is 85% water. Although the brain is only 2 percent of the total weight of the body, it uses 5 percent of the blood supply.

With dehydration, the level of energy generation in the brain is decreased. Depression and chronic fatigue syndrome are frequently results of dehydration.

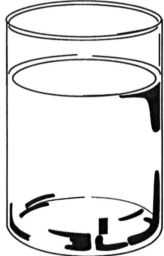

Seventy-five percent of Americans are chronically dehydrated.

Even mild dehydration will slow down one's metabolism as much as 3%.

Lack of water is the No. 1 trigger of daytime fatigue.

A mere 2% drop in body water can trigger fuzzy short-term memory, trouble with basic math and difficulty focusing on the computer screen or on a printed page.

A misbehaving child is often dehydrated.

Sources:

Your Body's Many Cries for Water, by Dr. F. Batmanghelidj

The Learning Brain, by Eric Jensen

Be Word Wise

Materials:

A chalkboard or flip chart

Goals:

— To learn how to reframe thoughts for a fresh approach
— To learn how to accept responsibility for our behavior with powerful language
— To learn that words can hurt or help a situation
— To learn how to adopt a more positive attitude

Set the Stage:

Ask the students, *How many of you have ever had someone tell you that you needed to improve your attitude?* (There are usually a lot hands that go up with this question.) *How do you do that? Would you like to know?*

Indicate to the students that they will see how changing their language can help change their attitudes.

Model:

Put the following lists on the chalkboard or a flip chart:

<u>Worn out thinking</u> *(Keeps us weak)*	<u>Reframed thinking for a fresh approach</u> *(Empowers us)*
They made me.	I chose to and I can choose something else.
I can't.	I can keep trying until I get it.
That's all we have is peanut butter, ugh!	I don't like peanut butter, but I guess it'll do.
No one understands me.	I need to understand myself.
It's hopeless.	I just need to find another way or ask for help.
You're always late!	Is there anything I can do to help you be on time?
Focuses on the past.	Focuses on solutions in the present.

Review the two lists with the students and discuss the differences between the two.

Explain that reframing means changing your thinking and language to have a different meaning.

Mini-Lecture and Questions:

Ask the students the following questions and lead a brief discussion.

How does reframing the statement change the outlook we have? What is the effect on us when we restate worn out thinking with a fresh approach? (It makes us feel more positive, confident and in control of our lives.)

Practice:

Let the students work in groups of four to come up with more examples of reframing. Ask volunteers to share their examples with the whole class.

Review:

Ask the students, *How can we use the concept of reframing to empower ourselves?*

Celebrate:

Acknowledge the students' efforts to reframe and refresh their worn-out thinking.

Nini the Cat

Materials:

The story, "Nini the Cat"
Art materials

Goals:

— To understand the root causes of anger
— To minimize aggressive or self-destructive behavior
— To promote a respect for and kindness toward animals

Set the Stage:

Ask the students, *Have you ever been angry and didn't know why you felt that way?* As the students share, share an example of you own. Tell the students that you are going to read them a story about misplaced anger.

Invite the students to listen to a story about Nini the cat.

Model:

Read the story, "Nini the Cat" to the class.

Mini-Lecture and Questions:

After reading the story, ask the following questions:

1. Why was the little boy hurting cats? (He was frustrated and angry.)
2. What was making him angry? (his inability to read)
3 What else was he feeling? (He was sad because he was being teased by others.)
4. What does it mean to displace anger? (You take your anger out on an innocent victim.)
5. How did the boy change the way he expressed his anger and frustration? (Nini the cat showed him how to express his anger by talking it out.)

Practice:

Let the students choose a way to illustrate the story. Examples, drawing a picture, writing a poem, writing another Nini the talking cat story, giving a presentation to the class using a toy cat as a prop.

Review:

Review by leading a discussion of the following questions, *What was the important lesson that the little boy learned from Nini?* (He learned to understand why he was angry and how to get help instead of displacing his anger onto the cats.) *Why should we respect animals? How will you use what you learned from this lesson?* (I will listen to my anger and resolve the problem rather than express my anger inappropriately.)

Celebrate:

Visit the local zoo or animal shelter. Invite a speaker from the zoo or animal shelter. Have weekly problem-solving meetings to address problems and feelings.

Nini the Cat

Once there was a little boy who liked to do very mean things to the helpless cats in the neighborhood. He would throw rocks at them, pull their tails and even throw them against the wall. He would then laugh and run away as if he felt better after these cruel acts.

One day, the boy was in the alley looking for a cat to tease. He saw a black furry cat a few feet away, and he decided to pick up a stone and throw it to frighten the cat. But this time, as he picked up the rock, a very strange thing happened. He heard a voice say, "Why are you so angry?"

"Who said that?" the boy asked.

"I did," said the cat as he walked up to the little boy and looked him in the eye.

"Why are you so angry? The cats around here certainly have not hurt you. So, why are you trying to hurt us?"

The little boy was amazed. He didn't know what to do, so he just stood there looking at the talking cat.

Then the cat spoke again, "Why don't you pick me up. I'm very soft and cuddly, and I think you could use a gentle touch. My name is Nini."

At first, the boy was afraid. But slowly he bent down and picked up the cat. The cat nuzzled the boy and purred in his arms. The boy felt the cat's heart beating, and began to stroke him. Suddenly, large tears began to run down the little boy's face.

"Why are you crying?" said Nini.

"I don't know," said the boy. "Not many people are as nice to me as you are. I can't read very well, and the kids at school tease me."

"I don't know why kids would tease you just because you need help with your reading," said Nini.

"Well, I haven't really asked anybody for help. When the teacher wants me to read, I just act silly and pick on other kids. I pretend to be mean, so they won't bother me."

Nini purred and said, "Gee, it sounds like you should tell your mom and dad what is going on, because you are taking your anger and frustration out on others who have nothing to do with your problem."

The little boy quietly told Nini more about himself. "My father is always busy working, and so is my mother. When they come home, they are so tired that I don't want to bother them. And, most of all, I don't want them to know that they have a stupid son."

"My my," said Nini, "I think we had better have a long talk."

Nini and the little boy sat for hours while Nini told the little boy how special he was.

Nini explained that the boy's mother and father were indeed busy, but they loved him very much and would certainly help him if he would only tell them about his anger and frustration. He also told the boy that his parents were working hard to buy things for him, but they would really want to know how they could help him in other ways too. Nini convinced the boy that he must give it a try and talk to his parents.

"Thank you so much," said the little boy to Nini. "I will talk to my parents. Won't you come home with me and be my cat?"

"Thank you for the offer, but I am used to roaming around freely," said Nini. "I think it would be nice if you went to the animal shelter and adopted a cat who needs a home."

Well, this story has a happy ending. The little boy's parents were so glad that he told them of his anger and frustration and inability to read well. They immediately went to the school, and with the help of the teacher, got tutoring and extra help for the little boy.

After that, the boy's reading and behavior improved in school. He started making friends, and his parents promised to slow down and communicate with him and with each other on a regular basis. However, the best thing that happened for the little boy was that he and his parents went to the local animal shelter and adopted a beautiful little kitten. You guessed it. Now the little boy has his own "Nini."

He never again wanted to hurt an animal. The boy even spoke to his classmates about being kind to animals and to each other. He taught his friends to ask for help just as Nini had taught him.

As for the original Nini, he is still prowling the alleys and teaching humans how to be more humane.

Part Three

Relationship Skills

Let no one come to you without leaving better and happier.
Be the living expression of kindness
Kindness in your smile,
Kindness in your eyes,
Kindness in your face.

Mother Teresa

Nature's Softening Influence

Materials:

The handout "The Old Lakota Was Wise"
Music tape or CD with nature sounds
Music of Native American flutes

Optional: Toy puppies and items from nature such as pine cones, leaves, flowers, etc.

Goals:

— To equate respect for nature and animals with respect for humans
— To experience the stress-relieving effects of nature
— To recognize, accept and appreciate diversity

Set the Stage:

Play music with nature sounds. Ask the students to close their eyes and get in touch with their feelings as you elaborate and describe each scene below. Allow time for the students to really experience each scene.
* Sitting under a large, green pine tree
* Sitting on a white sandy beach looking out at the ocean
* Walking in a beautiful flower garden
* Holding a cuddly, soft puppy

Ask the following questions:
— *Why do these images tend to soothe your mind and relax your body?*
— *How do nature and animals affect humans?* (They have a positive, stress-relieving effect.)

Model:

Give each student a copy of the handout "The Old Lakota Was Wise." Play Native American flute music while you read the quote of Chief Luther Standing Bear.

Mini-Lecture and Questions:

If possible, take the class outside to continue the lesson near grass and trees. If you can't go outside, bring nature inside by giving each student a pine cone, leaf, flower or toy puppy to hold as you ask the following questions:

1. What was Chief Luther Standing Bear telling us?

Relationship Skills

2. Do you agree with his message? Why or why not?
3. Why is it important to respect nature and animals? (We are connected to nature and animals in the web of life.)
4. How does respecting nature help us to respect other humans? (It teaches us to live in harmony with all people, nature and animals.)
5. How would a flower garden look if all the flowers were the same?
6. How might that remind us to appreciate differences in people?
7. Can the peacefulness we feel in nature help us find peace within ourselves by simply getting quiet or closing our eyes? (Yes, we can recall the peaceful feelings we had in nature no matter where we are, if we close our eyes and imagine ourselves back in that scene. We can even use this technique to calm ourselves before a test or in a stressful situation.)

Practice:

Let the students form groups to plan projects to help the environment. Examples:

- Start a recycling project at school or in the neighborhood.
- Visit other classes to speak about not littering the school grounds.
- Organize a group to clean up a park or someone's yard.
- Adopt a bus stop.
- Write to your legislator to advocate for environmental issues.
- Write poetry about nature and animals.
- Make posters encouraging students to keep school grounds litter free.
- Compose and record a song about the environment to raise money for the school. (Sell your song to parents and members of the community.)
- Donate money to the local zoo and or an animal rescue shelter.
- Present talks about the importance of being a responsible pet owner.
- Put on a play for the school and community about "Nature's Softening Influence."

Review:

As a large group, share what you have learned from this lesson. Tell how you will use this new understanding in your life.

Celebrate:

Schedule a special day to display and recognize the group projects. Invite parents, community members and peers. Let the students tell how working together with others made the projects successful.

Acknowledge that the joy of honoring the environment taught the students to honor themselves and one another.

Relationship Skills

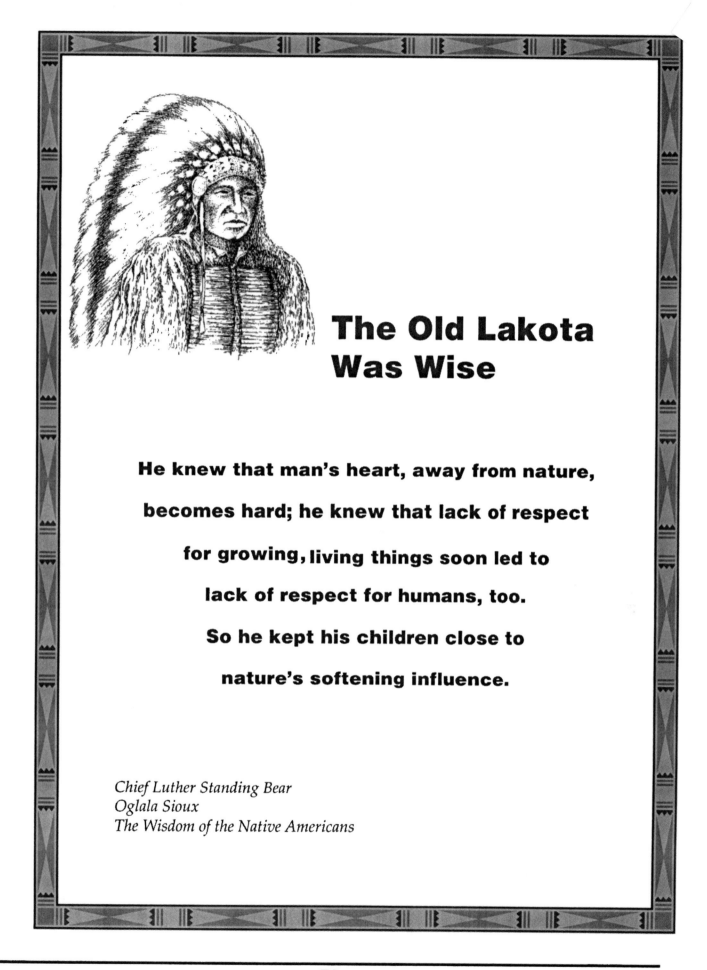

The Old Lakota Was Wise

He knew that man's heart, away from nature,

becomes hard; he knew that lack of respect

for growing, living things soon led to

lack of respect for humans, too.

So he kept his children close to

nature's softening influence.

Chief Luther Standing Bear
Oglala Sioux
The Wisdom of the Native Americans

The Coyote and the Race

Materials:

The story "The Coyote and the Race,"
Native American flute music such as "Canyon Trilogy" by Carlos Nakai

Goals:

— To recognize the advantages of cooperation
— To learn to work cooperatively as a team
— To recognize and respect one's feelings and needs and those of others

Set the Stage:

Ask the students:

— *Have you ever won a competition? How did it feel?*
— *Have you ever achieved a goal with a group of friends?*
— *How did these two experiences differ for you?*

Now explain that you'd like them to listen to a Native American folk tale about a competition.

Model:

Read the story "The Coyote and the Race." Play Native American flute music during the story to help set the mood.

At the completion of the story, have the students turn to the person closest to them and share what they thought the lesson was for Coyote.

Complete the story by sharing the following version of the lesson: In the race of life, every time we stop to help someone else, there is an instant victory and we all win.

Mini-Lecture and Questions:

Ask for volunteers to share with the large group what they shared with their partner. Allow time for the sharing of thoughts with the entire group.

Ask the large group:

1. How important is winning a competition to you?
2. What is the value of cooperation?

3. Is competition ever okay?
4. How did coyote feel when he won the first time?
5. Why was winning the second time more rewarding for him?
6. Would more cooperation among students and teachers benefit our school? How?

Practice:

Have the students get into groups of four or five and ask them to brainstorm ways to promote more cooperation in the classroom, in the school, in families, and in the world.

Review:

Let each group present their its ideas ¡to the class.

Celebrate:

Acknowledge the students' effort and assist them with implementing as many of the suggestions as possible. Celebrate the results in the school and community newspapers.

The Coyote and The Race

(Adapted from a Native American folk tale)

One day in the forest, there was to be a great race. All the animals were there. The animals who were racing were the coyote, the bear and the turtle. As the race began, the coyote knew that he was the fastest, and so he lay down for a nap. Some time later, he awoke in a panic. *I'm behind*, he thought. *I have to win the race.*

And so he took off down the road. Soon he came upon the bear, who was caught in a trap. "Help me, help me," cried the bear, but the coyote did not stop. He wanted to win the race.

A little farther down the road, coyote came upon the turtle. The turtle had flipped over on his back. "Help me, help me," cried the turtle. But, the coyote did not stop. He wanted to win the race.

Coyote finally crossed the finish line first, and he won the race. But he looked around and saw no one there to celebrate with him. And so he died of a great loneliness. As he went up to Grandfather Spirit, Grandfather Spirit said to him, "Coyote, I want you to go back and run that race again, but this time I want you to do it differently."

And so, coyote found himself running on the road again. This time, when he came to the bear caught in a trap, he stopped to help him, and off they hobbled down the road together. And when they saw the turtle and he said, "Help me," Coyote said, "Let's pick Mr. Turtle up and carry him with us." And so they did.

Once again, coyote crossed the finish line, but this time, he crossed it together with his friends, bear and turtle. Suddenly, all of the animals came out of the forest, and there was a great celebration!

Then Coyote turned to the other animals and said, "I learned a very important lesson today."

Communication Skills Can Improve Your Life!

Introduction:

Often, communication skills are taught in isolation, one skill at a time. In this lesson, we see the progression of skills. I have used this lesson successfully in elementary and high schools, and with adults. All have benefited from these lessons, but wouldn't it be great if everyone could learn these skills while they are still in elementary school?

Materials:

The handout "Communication Skills"

Goals:

— To learn the skills of sending and receiving communication effectively
— To learn to show empathy by acknowledging feelings in others
— To learn to prevent conflict through effective communication

Set the Stage:

Ask the students:

— *Who would like to have better relationships in their lives?*
— *What do you think can help improve relationships with others?* (the ability to communicate one's own feelings and to recognize the feelings of others)
— *Do you think that good communication skills can lessen tensions and prevent conflicts in relationships?* (Yes, they can.)

Tell the students that you'd like them to watch a roleplay and notice the communication skills of the participants.

Model:

The counselor or teacher and a volunteer model the following role-play:

Scene One —
   A student comes home from school. Mom is reading the paper. She says, "Hi, John. How was school today?"

Relationship Skills

John says, "It was terrible. I got in trouble and had to go to the principal."
Mother responds without looking up, "That's nice dear. I have a class at
   7:00 tonight. I'll see you later." (end of roleplay)

Ask the students what they noticed about the mother's communication skills.
(She wasn't really listening to John. She didn't look at him, and she was
absorbed in her own thoughts.) Next, ask them how they think John felt? (He
may have felt hurt, disappointed and even angry.) Finally, ask them if anyone
had ever communicated with them in this way and have they ever communicated to someone else like this? (Probably so. Most people have not had the
opportunity to learn effective listening skills.)

Now, ask them to look at the scene again with the mother now showing
effective listening skills.

Scene Two —

Repeat Scene One until you get to the mother's response.

   Mother's response: As she puts the newspaper down and looks at John,
      she says, "You had a terrible day? And you had to go to see the princi-
      pal? You sound really frustrated. Tell me more about what happened."
   After John tells her about his problem, mother responds again. She says,
      "It certainly does sound like you have a serious problem. What do you
      think you can do about it?"
   John says, "I don't know Mom, I want you to call the teacher and tell her
      that she was wrong to send me to the office. I didn't do anything!"
   Mom looks at John and says, "John, when you want me to solve your
      problem, I feel frustrated, because it puts the responsibility on me. I
      can help you, but I think you have the ability to solve this problem
      yourself. Let's think of some solutions." The roleplay ends.

Mini-Lecture and Questions:

Ask the students to think about the two different scenes as they begin to learn
about communication skills. Now ask,

   1. How did mother's response in Scene Two differ from Scene One? (She
      was a much better listener.)
   2. How do you think John felt after his mother's response in Scene Two?
      (He probably felt much better, because his mom showed sensitivity
      and caring.)
   3. Do you think he will want to share more about his problem with her?
      (Yes, people are more willing to talk with someone when they feel that
      the other person cares enough to listen well.)

Explain that empathy is the ability to understand someone else's feelings. John's mother was showing empathy in Scene Two. His mother also used several other effective listening skills that the students are now going to learn and practice.

Give each student a copy of the handout "Communications Skills." Using the handout, point out the skills the mother used.

- She repeated John's words. ("You had a bad day at school?")
- She listened to and acknowledged his feelings. ("You sound frustrated.")
- She asked for clarification or more information. ("Tell me more.")
- She helped him to explore ways to solve his problem. ("What do you think you can do about that?")
- She used an "I statement" to keep John from putting the responsibility for his problem on her. ("When you expect me to solve the problem, I feel frustrated, because it puts your responsibility on me.")

Practice:

Have the students get into groups of three. Let two of the students role-play Scene Two again while the third person observes and gives feedback. Person No. 3 makes sure that all five skills are used in the role-play. Have the students take turns being the mother so that they each can practice using the skills.

Let the students create another role-play in which they model the five communication skills.

Review:

Let the students generate three questions to be asked for a review of the lesson. Then make a poster of the handout and display it in a prominent place in the classroom.

Celebrate:

Acknowledge the students for making the effort to learn skills that will improve relationships in the classroom and in each student's personal life.

Follow up by reading the book *How To Win Friends and Influence People* to the class. Explain that the author, Dale Carnegie, was one of the best communicators of all times. Students of all generations will benefit from the principles in this book.

Communication Skills

1. **Repeat the words** -

    Like a parrot, repeat the words you heard the speaker say.
    This shows that you are listening.
    >   Examples: "So you had a bad day
    >   at school?""You had to go and see
    >   the principal?"

2. **Listen for feelings** -

    Acknowledge the person's feelings.
    >   Example: "You sound frustrated."

3. **Clarify** -

    Get a clearer understanding of the problem.
    >   Example: "Tell me more about what happened."

4. **Explore alternatives** -

    Consider options and solutions.
    >   Example: "What do you think you can do about that?"

5. **Use "I" statements** -

    Send clear communication of thoughts and feelings.
    >   Example: "When you expect me to solve the problem, I
    >   feel frustrated, because it puts the responsibility on
    >   me."

    When you_____I feel_____because_____.

Adapted from: *Systematic Training for Effective Parenting*

The Hula Hoop

Materials:

One Hula-Hoop or enough for the whole class (check with the P.E. department)
Any upbeat music

Goal:

— To understand personal rights, boundaries and the need for self-control

Set the Stage:

Have one student demonstrate the Hula-Hoop while you play music. If there are enough hoops for the whole class, let everyone play.

Give no hint that this is part of a lesson, and let them exercise with the hoops for about 10 minutes.

Model:

Stop the music and take one Hula-Hoop. Show how the Hula-Hoop creates a circle around your body.

Ask the students if, when you take the Hula-Hoop away, they can still imagine the circle around you.

Mini-Lecture and Questions:

Ask the students to give you a definition for the word "boundary" (a line that shows an area or territory). If you are working with young children, show a boundary line on a map.

Explain that we all have personal boundaries. Say to the students, "Think of your personal boundary as the space or area inside the hula-hoop that is around your waist.

"You have a right to your personal boundary. This means that it is not okay for someone to grab you, hit you or otherwise invade your personal boundary space.

"People can come within your personal boundary space, if you choose to let them, but you also have the responsibility to respect the personal boundary space of others. This means using self-control to avoid hurting someone else by inappropriately intruding on their personal boundary space. (This could be by touching, hitting, taking something from someone else, etc.)"

Relationship Skills

81

Explain that boundaries are also fluid and can change. Just as when the Hula-Hoop is circling around us, it is sometimes close to us and sometimes farther away. We have the right to choose when to let someone come close to us or when we prefer that they stay farther away. Acceptable boundaries can also vary among cultures.

It is important that we let people know when they are violating our personal boundaries.

Practice:

Put the students into groups of four or five and appoint a recorder for each group. Have the students suggest a list of ways to show respect for personal boundaries.

Here are some examples:

- Keep hands and feet to ourselves.
- Stay a comfortable distance from people when speaking with them.
- Respect the property of others.

The recorder records all of the suggestions. After 20 minutes, the recorders will share each group's list with the class by writing their lists on the board.

Let the students comment on the different lists.

Ask them to identify some common suggestions on all the lists. (Circle the common suggestions.)

Finally, help the class make one list of suggestions to post in the classroom. This can be put on a poster and displayed in the room.

Review:

Summarize by asking the following questions:

— *What have we learned from this lesson?*
— *How will you use what you have learned?*
— *Can your awareness of respect for personal boundaries help you in your relationships with others? How?* (Yes, other people have respect for me when I show respect for them, and I will prevent conflicts with others.)

Celebrate:

Start the music and continue with the hula- hoop fun. You may want to purchase and keep one hula-hoop in the classroom as a daily reminder to respect personal boundaries.

Rapport, Rapport, Rapport

Materials:

The story "The Watermelon Hunter"
A chalkboard or chart paper and pens

Goals:

— To understand personal rights, boundaries and the need for self-control
— To recognize, accept and appreciate individual differences and various points of view
— To recognize, accept and respect family, ethnic and cultural differences

Set the Stage:

Ask the students if they have ever thought they were helping someone by telling him or her the truth, and instead, the other person got mad at them?

Allow time for the students to share. Share a time when this happened to you, as well.

Model:

Read the story "The Watermelon Hunter" by Brian Cavanaugh, and ask the students to listen for its symbolic meaning.

Mini-Lecture and Questions:

Ask the students to think about the hidden message in this story. Then ask them the following questions and lead a brief discussion.

1. What was the "monster" that the villagers were afraid of? (a watermelon)
2. Why were the villagers afraid of the first traveler? (because he killed the monster, and they were afraid he would kill them, too)

Explain that the traveler thought that he was doing the villagers a favor by showing them the truth about the monster — that it was only a melon.

3. What mistake did he make? (The villagers did not know him and trust him, and they were not ready to believe what he told them. He didn't take the time to get to know the villagers' beliefs.)
4. How did the second traveler gain the trust of the villagers? (He went to live with them and came to know them. As they spent time with him

Relationship Skills

83

and learned to know him, they became willing to listen to what he had to say and show to them.)

Tell the students that having a good relationship with someone means having good rapport with them. Rapport means understanding and respecting another's point of view. This is true whether it is between two people, two groups or two countries.

Go on to explain that we live in a very diverse world. For example, there are people of varying cultures, races, genders and religions. With these differences come different customs, values and points of view. If we don't take the time to understand someone who is different from us, we can create conflict by simply not knowing how to relate to the other person.

Practice:

Put the students in pairs and ask them to share why building rapport is important when meeting new people. (With diversity comes differences of beliefs, opinions and customs.)

Ask the students to tell their partners how their partners could build rapport with them. Allow them to talk for 10 minutes and then ask for volunteers to share with the large group what they shared with their partners.

Review:

Ask the students to identify some things they can do to build rapport with others. List examples on the board or on chart paper.

Ask for volunteers to role-play some of their suggestions. Examples might include finding out about others' likes and dislikes, being a good listener, not trying to impose your views before you know how they will be received, developing trust, knowing that it takes time, being genuinely interested in getting to know the other person(s), and studying other cultures, religions, etc., to become more informed.

Celebrate:

Acknowledge the students' efforts. Add the suggestions for building rapport to the list of new communication skills and post it for all to see.

Invite guest speakers from different cultures to come to the class and teach the students about their customs and beliefs.

The Watermelon Hunter

by Brian Cavanaugh

Once upon a time, there was a man who strayed from his own country into the world known as the Land of Fools. He soon saw a number of people flying in terror from a field where they had been trying to reap wheat. "There is a monster in that field," they told him. He looked and saw that the "monster" was merely a watermelon.

He offered to kill the "monster" for them. When he had cut the melon from its stalk, he took a slice and began to eat it. The people became even more terrified of him than they had been of the melon. They drove him away with pitchforks, crying, "He will kill us next, unless we get rid of him!"

It so happened that shortly afterward another man also strayed into the Land of Fools. But instead of offering to help the people with the "monster," he agreed with them that it must be dangerous, and by tiptoeing away from it with them, he gained their confidence. He spent a long time with them in their homes until he could teach them, little by little, the basic facts that would enable them not only to lose their fear of melons but eventually to culti-vate melons themselves.

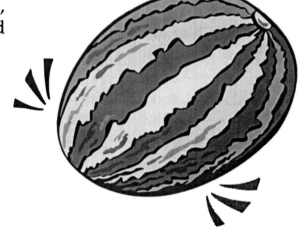

Peace Pilgrim

Introduction:

I have included a lesson on Peace Pilgrim, because she has been a great inspiration in my life. Peace Pilgrim was a woman who gave up all of her worldly possessions and traveled alone teaching people about inner peace. She walked more than 25,000 miles across the United States, Canada and Mexico talking to individuals and groups, and showing them how to resolve problems that they were having in their lives by adopting a peaceful strategy or attitude. All along the way, she was fed and housed by generous people who believed in her cause. Peace Pilgrim felt that if all people could develop inner peace, it would lead to peace in communities and throughout the world. There are now over 200 Peace Pilgrim centers around the world. The centers send out books and pamphlets on Peace Pilgrim to anyone who asks for them. All of the materials are free. Many people, however, make donations to the centers to help carry on the work of Peace Pilgrim.

For information, books or materials, contact:
Friends of Peace Pilgrim
7350 Dorado Canyon Road
Somerset, CA 95684
www.peacepilgrim.com

Materials:

The handout "Peace Pilgrim"
The CD "Let There Be Peace on Earth" (A good version is by Vince Gil.)

Goals:

— To teach the students about the life of Peace Pilgrim
— To promote non-violent conflict resolution
— To help the students understand the value of inner peace

Set the Stage:

Ask the students if they know what a pilgrim is. (someone who makes a journey on behalf of a cause)

Explain that this lesson is about a pilgrim for peace, a woman who became known as "Peace Pilgrim."

Model:

Give each student a copy of the handout "Peace Pilgrim."

Ask the students to follow along as you read the quote.

Mini-Lecture and Questions:

After reading the quote, ask the students:

1. Does anyone know about the life of Peace Pilgrim? (Read the introduction to the students as a way to introduce them to the life and work of Peace Pilgrim.)
2. After hearing a little bit about Peace Pilgrim and reading her quote, what do you think she meant in the quote? (If our objective in solving the problem is to resolve the issue and not "win" the argument, we are more apt to find a quick and peaceful solution.)

Explain that Peace Pilgrim advocated solving conflicts in a way that everyone's needs were met, and she was very successful at doing this. She was not associated with any religion or organization. She spoke for herself and had much wisdom and insight to share. She died in 1981 in a car accident.

3. Have you ever taken the approach that Peace Pilgrim teaches in solving your own problems? Can you give us an example?

Give the students time to share examples.

4. What can you do when you find yourself in a conflict so that you can remember and use the advice of Peace Pilgrim? (I can remember that my goal is to solve the problem and not to try to gain the advantage over the other person.)

Practice:

Have the students create a book of poems, quotes or stories on positive approaches to peace just as the Friends of Peace Pilgrim have done. Duplicate the book so that each student has a copy. Then let the class brainstorm ways to get Peace Pilgrim's message out to classmates, families and the community by donating their book to as many places as possible. (Be sure to send one to the Friends of Peace Pilgrim.)

Review:

Let the whole class talk about ways to have a more peaceful classroom, community and world. (Suggest that they send for and read Peace Pilgrim's book, *Peace Pilgrim, In Her Own Words*, and the booklet, *Steps to Inner Peace* (available from Friends of Peace Pilgrim).

Celebrate:

Acknowledge the students' peace efforts in the school and community newspapers. Often, it is only the violent acts that make the news. Encourage the students by recognizing them for positive actions.

Conclude the activity by singing the song "Let There Be Peace On Earth" and/or playing the CD.

Peace Pilgrim

"There is a magic formula for resolving conflicts. It is this: Have as your objective the resolving of the conflict, not the gaining of advantage.

"There is a magic formula for avoiding conflicts. It is this: Be concerned that you do not offend, not that you are not offended."

Shades of Color

Introduction:

"What Color is Skin?" is one of the best children's films I've found for learning about racial differences. Although this film was designed for the elementary level, I have used it in middle and high school. One way to heighten the students' awareness is to ask some of the questions in the guide before viewing. I found very few teens who knew what melanin was, why people get a suntan, or how the races are similar and different.

Materials:

The video "What Color is Skin?" Available for purchase from: Pyramid Films Corp., 2801 Colorado Ave., Santa Monica, CA 90404, phone: (310) 828-7577 — Cost: $79 (Check with your school district. They may have it available.)

Goals:

— To recognize, accept and respect racial differences
— To understand the concept of race

Set the Stage:

To tee the students up for viewing the video, ask the following two questions:

— Do you know why we have different races of people?
— Are people different colors or just different shades of the same color?

Tell the students that these questions will be answered in a film that they are about to see, and that they will discuss the questions after the film.

Model:

Show the film "What Color is Skin?"

Mini-Lecture and Questions:

Follow the film guide.

Practice:

Assign the students the project of researching their ancestry and preparing a brief biography. Encourage them to use the library, the Internet, interviews of parents and relatives, and other sources they may find. Assign a completion date.

Review:

When the projects are completed, have the students each give a brief presentation on his or her ancestry.

Celebrate:

Celebrate the completion of the projects. Acknowledge the wonderful diversity in the group and celebrate the joy of diversity by marking on a calendar the holidays or celebrations for the different cultural or racial groups in the class. Acknowledge and celebrate as many of the holidays as possible. Let the students decide the best ways to celebrate the holidays.

The Web of Life

Materials:

A spider web drawn on a large piece of paper or purchased at a craft shop
Pictures brought in by the students of their families, friends and themselves
Ribbon or small craft clothespins to attach the pictures to the web or glue if using a picture of a spider web
A ball of heavy string
The handout quote by Chief Seattle

Note: This is a good activity to do in October when stores are selling spider webs for Halloween.

Goal:

— To recognize, accept and respect the connection of all people, animals and nature

Set the Stage:

Ask the students:

— What is a web? (a network of carefully woven, connected parts)
— What kinds of webs are there? (spider webs, the World Wide Web)

Tell the students that there is also the imaginary "Web of Life." This is the symbolic web that connects all people, animals and nature together on this Earth.

Model:

Help the students visualize and feel the connection of a web with the following activity.

Have the students get into a circle.

Take the ball of string and throw it to a student. That student is to hold on to the end of the string but throw the ball to another student who is to hold onto his or her part of the string and then throw the ball to another student. This continues until every student in the circle is holding onto the string. As the ball weaves its way back and forth across the circle, an intricate web is woven.

While the students continue to hold onto their parts of the web, ask them to step back an inch or two to tighten the web. Then direct the students on one

Relationship Skills

side of the web to slightly lift their side. Have the students notice what happens to the other side? (It moves, too.)

Go to another part of the web and repeat the process. Then ask everyone to let go of the web and take their seats.

Mini-Lecture and Questions:

Give each student a copy of the quote by Chief Seattle and allow silent reading. Ask the students:

1. After experiencing the web activity and reading Chief Seattle's quote, what do you think Chief Seattle was saying to us?
2. Do you agree with him? Why or why not?
3. If we believe what Chief Seattle is saying, why should we never harm another person, animal or the environment? (because what we do to others affects us as well, just as when we lifted one side of our string web and the other side moved.)
4. How does Chief Seattle's quote relate to the Golden Rule — "Treat others the way that you would like them to treat you."? (When we treat others the way that we would like to be treated, we are acknowledging our connectedness.)

Practice:

Tell the students that they are going to make a display of their own web of life.

Have the students take the pictures they brought to class and attach them to the web to make an interesting picture display. If the web is drawn on paper, the students can glue or paste pictures onto it.

When creating a three-dimensional web, I have used a hole punch to put a hole at the top of the picture and tied it with pretty string to the web.

You may also want to purchase decorative mini-clothespins from a craft store and attach the pictures in that way. Another idea is to tie a beautiful feather onto the web. The students can also add pictures of stranger and animals, and nature scenes.

Review:

Have the students share their webs with each other. Encourage them to describe their pictures. Then create a display in the room with all of the webs.

Place the webs so that they are touching or connected, and point out that you have created one connected "Web of Life."

Celebrate:

Either on the same day or soon after the webs have been made, celebrate with a "Web of Life" feast. Let each student bring in food and/or music that represents his or her culture. Note that food and music are two of the things that unite all people in the "Web of Life."

The Web of Life

We are but one thread
Within the web of life.
Whatever we do to the web,
We do to ourselves.

For all things are
Bound together.
All things connect.

Chief Seattle

What's Your Style?

Materials:

An age-appropriate learning styles inventory (many are available on the Internet or from your school district)
A video on learning styles (available from Learning Forum Success Products, (800) 527-5321. You may also check with the special education department. They may have these materials.)

Goal:

— To apply knowledge of learning styles to positively influence school performance

Set the Stage:

Ask the students,

— *Have you ever seen a fashion show?*
— *What was being shown?* (different styles of clothes that people prefer to wear)

Explain to the students that they are going to have a different kind of fashion show in class today. It will show different ways or styles in which the students prefer to learn.

Model:

Say to the students: *We all learn visually, with our eyes; auditorily, with our ears; and kinesthetically by touching or doing an activity. Kinesthetic learning also means involving our emotions by making the learning fun, exciting and meaningful. Even though we all learn in all of these ways, we are going to find out today how we like to learn best.*

I'm going to give you an easy questionnaire so you can learn some important things about yourself.

Administer the learning styles inventory.

Mini-Lecture and Questions:

After all the students have finished the inventory and considered the results, ask the following questions:

1. Are the results of the survey similar to what you know about yourself

as a learner? In other words, do you learn easily by hearing information? Do you learn by seeing a picture of something, or do you like to learn with activities and group interaction?

2. How can knowing the way you prefer to learn help you with school-work and homework? (I can study with all three styles but especially with my preferred learning style.)

Tell the students that they are now going to watch a video that will teach them more about learning styles. (Show the video.)

Practice:

After viewing the video, the students will have a better understanding of learning styles.

Next, tell the students that they are now going to have their own fashion show, which will demonstrate what they have learned. Add that in this fashion show, rather than featuring styles of clothing, styles of learning are going to be featured.

Let each student demonstrate his or her learning style by teaching the class something in their preferred learning style. Encourage the students to be creative. Examples may include the following:

- If someone is primarily visual, have him or her teach the lesson with pictures.
- If someone is primarily auditory, have him or her talk to the class about themselves.
- If the student is primarily kinesthetic, let him or her engage the class in a learning activity.

The students may also group by learning styles and do a presentation to-gether. The presentation is entitled: "Something I'd Like You To Know About Me." (This is a suggestion. Other titles can be chosen.)

You should circulate and assist the students with ideas for their presentations.

Finally, let the students demonstrate learning in all three learning styles in one lesson. Have them teach their lessons again, and this time have them incorporate all three learning styles into¡ the same lesson. For example: I can tell something about myself, show pictures of me, and then do a dance, sing my favorite song, or have the class play one of my favorite games.

Now, explain to the students that they have just experienced learning in three different styles.

Relationship Skills

Ask which of the two lessons that each student presented they will tend to remember. (The one in which they used all three learning styles to help us get to know one another.)

Let the students comment on the experience.

Review:

Remind the students that the best way to learn something is to study it in all three learning styles. That will ensure the best chance of success. We also should be understanding of others when their style does not match ours.

One style is not better than another. It's just the way our brains work.

Ask the students how, with their new knowledge of learning styles, they might better study for a history or spelling test, or a test in any other subject.

Also ask them how they might help someone who is being teased because he or she learn faster or slower than others. (Share with the person being teased and the teasers what you know about learning styles. Encourage them to be tolerant of one another.)

Celebrate:

Acknowledge the students for getting "out of their comfort zones" to have fun with this activity. Monitor and acknowledge improved grades as the students use their knowledge of learning styles to improve their study habits.

Focus on Solutions, Not Problems

Introduction:

I have included a video clip from the movie "Patch Adams" because it is a powerful demonstration of focusing so hard on a problem that the solution is missed. In schools, educators often react to the problems students exhibit while missing the underlying causes and appropriate solutions. Students also can engage the educators, their parents and themselves so deeply in a problem that they overlook their own ability to find solutions. This is a lesson for students and adults alike to remind them that the solutions to problems are there, if we will just take the time to see, hear and feel them. Please view the video before showing it to the class because the entire video is not appropriate for school-aged children. Cue the video to the segment where Patch is visiting with Arthur and Arthur teaches Patch the lesson of the four fingers. This segment is at the beginning of the video.

Materials:

The video "Patch Adams" (available at most video stores)
The handout "Six Steps to Effective Problem Solving and Decision Making"

Goals:

— To see the value of being focused on solutions
— To better focus on the task at hand and pay attention
— To learn an effective problem solving and decision making model

Set the Stage:

Write the following expression where the students will see it: "He can't see the forest for the trees."

Ask the students if anyone knows what this means. (By focusing so hard on a tree, he can't see the bigger picture of the whole forest. In other words, if we spend all of our energy "focusing" on a problem, we limit our ability to "see" a solution or many solutions.)

Ask the students if they can you give an example of a time when they experienced this. It will be helpful if you provide an example of your own.

Relationship Skills

Model:

Have the students watch the scene from the movie "Patch Adams." Explain that it illustrates this point very well.

Mini-Lecture and Questions:

Ask the students why they think Arthur gave "Patch" the following advice: "Look beyond the problem. Never focus on the problem. You can't see the solutions, if you focus on the problems. See what no one else sees. See the whole world anew each day."

Discuss how focusing on the problem keeps us in a crisis mode shutting down our ability to do our best thinking and find creative solutions. "See the world anew each day" reminds us to be open to new ways of thinking and seeing our world.

Flexibility means that when something is not working for us, we can try other options instead of continually doing the same thing over and over and getting the same results. There also might be multiple solutions.

Practice:

Give the students the handout, "Six Steps to Effective Problem Solving and Decision Making."

Have the students work in pairs to identify a problem they are having, and using the problem-solving model, to think of appropriate solutions. Be as creative as possible. "See what no one else sees."

Let the students share their problems and solutions with the larger group.

Review:

Let the students suggest three or four questions to review this lesson. Note that this model can also be used as a decision-making model by exploring options or alternative choices instead of "causes" of problems.

Celebrate:

Congratulate the students for expanding the way they look at their world.

Let them brainstorm and implement a creative solution to a community problem. For example, adopt a bus stop. Individuals or groups can clean up the neighborhood and make the bus stop a pleasant place by keeping it attractive.

Acknowledge the students' efforts in the school and community newspapers.

Relationship Skills

Six Steps to Effective Problem Solving And Decision Making

One: Identify the problem (or decision to be made).

Two: Consider possible causes of the problem (consider choices or options).

Three: Take three deep breaths. Relax and think about what you want and need.

Four: Focus on solutions. Look beyond the problem or the decision.

Five: Choose the solution or option that feels, seems and looks right for you.

Six: If that solution was not the best for you, go back to step one, ask for help, or just choose again.

Remember that we learn from our mistakes as well as from our successes. Learn from the mistake and make a better choice the next time. There also may be multiple solutions — be open to more than just one answer!

Part Four

School Counseling Program Standards and Student Competencies

Activity Matrix

Part One – Self Awareness

ACADEMIC DEVELOPMENT: Students will …

Activities	The Comfort Zone	Café EQ	Our Powerful Thoughts	Affirmations	The Choice is Yours	I Am Somebody	Be Careful Your Thoughts	Life is a Balancing Act
Standard A (…become effective learners)								
1. Display positive interest and pride in achievement.								
2. Articulate feelings of competence and confidence as a learner.						x		
3. Identify attitudes that lead to successful learning.	x	x	x			x	x	x
4. Use communication skills to know when and how to ask for help.								
5. Demonstrate the ability to work independently as well as cooperatively in groups.							x	x
6. Take responsibility for their actions.	x	x		x			x	x
7. Apply organization and time management skills.					x			
8. Demonstrate how effort and persistence positively affect learning.		x						
9. Apply knowledge of learning styles to positively influence school performance.								
Standard B (…plan to achieve goals)								
1. Demonstrate motivation to achieve individual potential.			x	x		x		
2. Learn and apply critical thinking skills.			x					
3. Seek, organize and apply academic information from a variety of sources.								
4. Apply knowledge of aptitudes, interest and learning styles to goal setting.								
5. Develop academic goals and an educational plan.					x			
6. Use decision-making and problem solving skills to enhance academic progress.								
7. Become independent and self-directed learners.								
Standard C (…relate school to life experiences)								
1. Understand the relationship between learning and work.								x
2. Demonstrate the ability to balance school, after-school activities and family life.								x
3. Seek community experience which will enhance school experiences.								
4. Demonstrate an understanding of the value of life-long learning.								
5. Understand how school success and academic achievement enhance future education, career and vocational opportunities.								x

CAREER DEVELOPMENT: Students will …

Activities	The Comfort Zone	Café EQ	Our Powerful Thoughts	Affirmations	The Choice is Yours	I Am Somebody	Be Careful Your Thoughts	Life is a Balancing Act
Standard A (…develop career awareness)								
1. Develop an awareness of personal abilities, skills, interests and motivators.		x				x		x
2. Develop a positive attitude towards work and learning.								x
3. Pursue and develop areas of interest.								
4. Learn how to work cooperatively in teams.								
5. Understand the importance of responsibility, attendance, punctuality, integrity and effort in the school setting.								
6. Learn to respect individual uniqueness at school and in the workplace.								
7. Demonstrate an understanding of the changing workplace.								
8. Learn to set goals and make decisions.					x			
9. Learn about the importance of planning and time-management skills.					x			
Standard B (…develop future career goals)								
1. Identify personal interests, abilities and relate them to various career options.						x		
2. Demonstrate awareness of the education needed to achieve career goals.								
3. Demonstrate awareness of traditional and nontraditional roles.								
4. Understand how changing economic and social needs influence future training and career.								
5. Understand the various ways careers can be classified.								
6. Use various resources, including the Internet to gain career information.								
7. Develop an educational plan to support career awareness.								
Standard C (…acquire career information)								
1. Understand the relationship between educational achievement and career success.								x
2. Understand that the changing workplace requires life-long learning and acquisition of new skills.								
3. Understand the effect of work on lifestyles.								
4. Understand the importance of equity and access in career choices.								
5. Learn to work cooperatively in teams and use conflict management skills.								
6. Understand that work is an important and satisfying means of personal expression.								x

PERSONAL/SOCIAL DEVELOPMENT: Students will …

Standard A (…acquire interpersonal skills)

Activities	The Comfort Zone	Café EQ	Our Powerful Thoughts	Affirmations	The Choice is Yours	I Am Somebody	Be Careful Your Thoughts	Life is a Balancing Act
1. Develop a positive attitude towards self as a unique and worthy person.	x							
2. Identify values, attitudes and beliefs.	x		x		x		x	
3. Identify and express feelings.		x		x	x	x	x	
4. Distinguish between appropriate and inappropriate behavior.		x	x				x	
5. Understand personal rights, boundaries and the need for self-control.								
6. Identify personal strengths and assets.				x		x		x
7. Use effective communication skills.								
8. Learn to make and keep friends.								
9. Recognize, accept and appreciate individual differences and various points of view.								
10. Recognize, accept and respect family, ethnic and cultural differences.								

Standard B (…make decisions, set goals)

Activities	The Comfort Zone	Café EQ	Our Powerful Thoughts	Affirmations	The Choice is Yours	I Am Somebody	Be Careful Your Thoughts	Life is a Balancing Act
1. Use decision-making or problem-solving model to understand consequences of choices.					x			
2. Develop effective coping skills.								
3. Demonstrate when, where, and how to seek help for solving problems.								
4. Know how to apply conflict resolution skills.								
5. Demonstrate a respect and appreciation for individual and cultural differences.								
6. Know when peer pressure is influencing a decision.								
7. Identify long- and short-term goals.					x			
8. Develop an action plan to set and achieve realistic goals.					x			x

Standard C (…acquire personal safety skills)

Activities	The Comfort Zone	Café EQ	Our Powerful Thoughts	Affirmations	The Choice is Yours	I Am Somebody	Be Careful Your Thoughts	Life is a Balancing Act
1. Demonstrate knowledge of information, emergency contact, etc. needed for personal safety.								
2. Learn about the relationship between appropriate and inappropriate physical contact.								
3. Learn about the relationship between rules, laws, safety and the protection of individual rights.								
4. Demonstrate the ability to assert boundaries, rights and personal privacy.								
5. Identify resource people in the school and community and how to seek support and help.								
6. Apply effective problem-solving and decision-making skills to make safe and healthy choices.								
7. Learn about the physical and emotional damages of alcohol and other drug use and abuse.								
8. Learn techniques for handling stress and coping with conflict to manage life events.		x						

Part Two — Managing Emotions

Activities	The Magic Doll	Persistence Pays Off	I Can Laugh At Me	Anger: Use It and Lose It	Inner and Outer Power	Tea Pot Talks	Music Sets The Mood	It's True: You Are What You Eat	Be Word Wise	Nini The Cat
ACADEMIC DEVELOPMENT: Students will …										
Standard A (…become effective learners)										
1. Display positive interest and pride in achievement.										
2. Articulate feelings of competence and confidence as a learner.										
3. Identify attitudes that lead to successful learning.		X			X	X				
4. Use communication skills to know when and how to ask for help.				X						
5. Demonstrate the ability to work independently as well as cooperatively in groups.						X				
6. Take responsibility for their actions.		X	X	X	X	X	X	X	X	X
7. Apply organization and time management skills.										
8. Demonstrate how effort and persistence positively affect learning.		X								
9. Apply knowledge of learning styles to positively influence school performance.										
Standard B (…plan to achieve goals)										
1. Demonstrate motivation to achieve individual potential.										
2. Learn and apply critical thinking skills.										
3. Seek, organize and apply academic information from a variety of sources.										
4. Apply knowledge of aptitudes, interest and learning styles to goal setting.										
5. Develop academic goals and an educational plan.										
6. Use decision-making and problem solving skills to enhance academic progress.										
7. Become independent and self-directed learners.										
Standard C (…relate school to life experiences)										
1. Understand the relationship between learning and work.										
2. Demonstrate the ability to balance school, after-school activities and family life.										
3. Seek community experience which will enhance school experiences.										
4. Demonstrate an understanding of the value of life-long learning.										
5. Understand how school success and academic achievement enhance future education, career and vocational opportunities.										

Activities

CAREER DEVELOPMENT: Students will …	The Magic Doll	Persistence Pays Off	I Can Laugh At Me	Anger: Use It and Lose It	Inner and Outer Power	Tea Pot Talks	Music Sets The Mood	It's True: You Are What You Eat	Be Word Wise	Nini The Cat
Standard A (...develop career awareness)										
1. Develop an awareness of personal abilities, skills, interests and motivators.		x				x				
2. Develop a positive attitude towards work and learning.		x					x			
3. Pursue and develop areas of interest.										
4. Learn how to work cooperatively in teams.		x				x				
5. Understand the importance of responsibility, attendance, punctuality, integrity and effort in the school setting.										
6. Learn to respect individual uniqueness at school and in the workplace.										
7. Demonstrate an understanding of the changing workplace.										
8. Learn to set goals and make decisions.										
9. Learn about the importance of planning and time-management skills.										
Standard B (...develop future career goals)										
1. Identify personal interests, abilities and relate them to various career options.										
2. Demonstrate awareness of the education needed to achieve career goals.										
3. Demonstrate awareness of traditional and nontraditional roles.										
4. Understand how changing economic and social needs influence future training and career.										
5. Understand the various ways careers can be classified.										
6. Use various resources, including the Internet to gain career information.										
7. Develop an educational plan to support career awareness.										
Standard C (...acquire career information)										
1. Understand the relationship between educational achievement and career success.										
2. Understand that the changing workplace requires life-long learning and acquisition of new skills.										
3. Understand the effect of work on lifestyles.										
4. Understand the importance of equity and access in career choices.										
5. Learn to work cooperatively in teams and use conflict management skills.										
6. Understand that work is an important and satisfying means of personal expression.										

Activities	The Magic Doll	Persistence Pays Off	I Can Laugh At Me	Anger: Use It and Lose It	Inner and Outer Power	Tea Pot Talks	Music Sets The Mood	It's True: You Are What You Eat	Be Word Wise	Nini The Cat
PERSONAL/SOCIAL DEVELOPMENT: Students will …										
Standard A (…acquire interpersonal skills)										
1. Develop a positive attitude towards self as a unique and worthy person.	×	×				×			×	×
2. Identify values, attitudes and beliefs.	×					×				×
3. Identify and express feelings.	×			×		×				×
4. Distinguish between appropriate and inappropriate behavior.				×	×	×			×	×
5. Understand personal rights, boundaries and the need for self-control.				×						×
6. Identify personal strengths and assets.										
7. Use effective communication skills.			×	×		×			×	×
8. Learn to make and keep friends.						×				
9. Recognize, accept and appreciate individual differences and various points of view.						×				
10. Recognize, accept and respect family, ethnic and cultural differences.										
Standard B (…make decisions, set goals)										
1. Use decision-making or problem-solving model to understand consequences of choices.	×									
2. Develop effective coping skills.										
3. Demonstrate when, where, and how to seek help for solving problems.						×			×	
4. Know how to apply conflict resolution skills.					×					
5. Demonstrate a respect and appreciation for individual and cultural differences.										
6. Know when peer pressure is influencing a decision.										
7. Identify long- and short-term goals.										
8. Develop an action plan to set and achieve realistic goals.								×		
Standard C (…acquire personal safety skills)										
1. Demonstrate knowledge of information, emergency contact, etc. needed for personal safety.										
2. Learn about the relationship between appropriate and inappropriate physical contact.										
3. Learn about the relationship between rules, laws, safety and the protection of individual rights.										
4. Demonstrate the ability to assert boundaries, rights and personal privacy.										×
5. Identify resource people in the school and community and how to seek support and help.										×
6. Apply effective problem-solving and decision-making skills to make safe and healthy choices.										
7. Learn about the physical and emotional damages of alcohol and other drug use and abuse.								×		
8. Learn techniques for handling stress and coping with conflict to manage life events.	×									

Part Three – Relationship Skills

ACADEMIC DEVELOPMENT: Students will …

Activities / Students will …	Focus on Solutions/ Not Problems	What's Your Style?	The Web of Life	Shades of Color	The Peace Pilgrim	Raport, Rapport, Rapport	The Hula Hoop	Communication Skills	The Coyote and The Race	Nature's Softening Influence
Standard A (…become effective learners)										
1. Display positive interest and pride in achievement.										
2. Articulate feelings of competence and confidence as a learner.										
3. Identify attitudes that lead to successful learning.	x		x	x	x	x			x	x
4. Use communication skills to know when and how to ask for help.								x		
5. Demonstrate the ability to work independently as well as cooperatively in groups.									x	
6. Take responsibility for their actions.								x	x	x
7. Apply organization and time management skills.										
8. Demonstrate how effort and persistence positively affect learning.									x	
9. Apply knowledge of learning styles to positively influence school performance.		x								
Standard B (…plan to achieve goals)										
1. Demonstrate motivation to achieve individual potential.										
2. Learn and apply critical thinking skills.	x									
3. Seek, organize and apply academic information from a variety of sources.										
4. Apply knowledge of aptitudes, interest and learning styles to goal setting.										
5. Develop academic goals and an educational plan.										
6. Use decision-making and problem solving skills to enhance academic progress.										
7. Become independent and self-directed learners.										
Standard C (…relate school to life experiences)										
1. Understand the relationship between learning and work.										
2. Demonstrate the ability to balance school, after-school activities and family life.										x
3. Seek community experience which will enhance school experiences.										x
4. Demonstrate an understanding of the value of life-long learning.										
5. Understand how school success and academic achievement enhance future education, career and vocational opportunities.										

CAREER DEVELOPMENT: Students will …

Activities	Nature's Softening Influence	The Coyote and The Race	Communication Skills	The Hula Hoop	Raport, Rapport, Rapport	The Peace Pilgrim	Shades of Color	The Web of Life	What's Your Style?	Focus on Solutions/ Not Problems
Standard A (…develop career awareness)										
1. Develop an awareness of personal abilities, skills, interests and motivators.										
2. Develop a positive attitude towards work and learning.	x									x
3. Pursue and develop areas of interest.										
4. Learn how to work cooperatively in teams.	x	x	x		x			x		
5. Understand the importance of responsibility, attendance, punctuality, integrity and effort in the school setting.										
6. Learn to respect individual uniqueness at school and in the workplace.	x							x	x	
7. Demonstrate an understanding of the changing workplace.										
8. Learn to set goals and make decisions.										
9. Learn about the importance of planning and time-management skills.										
Standard B (…develop future career goals)										
1. Identify personal interests, abilities and relate them to various career options.	x									
2. Demonstrate awareness of the education needed to achieve career goals.										
3. Demonstrate awareness of traditional and nontraditional roles.										
4. Understand how changing economic and social needs influence future training and career.										
5. Understand the various ways careers can be classified.										
6. Use various resources, including the Internet to gain career information.										
7. Develop an educational plan to support career awareness.										
Standard C (…acquire career information)										
1. Understand the relationship between educational achievement and career success.										
2. Understand that the changing workplace requires life-long learning and acquisition of new skills.										
3. Understand the effect of work on lifestyles.										
4. Understand the importance of equity and access in career choices.								x		
5. Learn to work cooperatively in teams and use conflict management skills.										
6. Understand that work is an important and satisfying means of personal expression.										

112

Part Three – Relationship Skills

Page 3 of 3

PERSONAL/SOCIAL DEVELOPMENT: Students will …

Activities	Nature's Softening Influence	The Coyote and The Race	Communication Skills	The Hula Hoop	Raport, Rapport, Rapport	The Peace Pilgrim	Shades of Color	The Web of Life	What's Your Style?	Focus on Solutions/Not Problems
Standard A (…acquire interpersonal skills)										
1. Develop a positive attitude towards self as a unique and worthy person.	x		x			x				
2. Identify values, attitudes and beliefs.					x					
3. Identify and express feelings.										
4. Distinguish between appropriate and inappropriate behavior.	x		x	x	x	x				
5. Understand personal rights, boundaries and the need for self-control.				x	x					
6. Identify personal strengths and assets.										
7. Use effective communication skills.			x							
8. Learn to make and keep friends.		x			x					
9. Recognize, accept and appreciate individual differences and various points of view.	x	x			x		x	x		
10. Recognize, accept and respect family, ethnic and cultural differences.	x				x		x	x		
Standard B (…make decisions, set goals)										
1. Use decision-making or problem-solving model to understand consequences of choices.										x
2. Develop effective coping skills.										
3. Demonstrate when, where, and how to seek help for solving problems.										
4. Know how to apply conflict resolution skills.						x				
5. Demonstrate a respect and appreciation for individual and cultural differences.	x						x	x		
6. Know when peer pressure is influencing a decision.										
7. Identify long- and short-term goals.										
8. Develop an action plan to set and achieve realistic goals.										
Standard C (…acquire personal safety skills)										
1. Demonstrate knowledge of information, emergency contact, etc. needed for personal safety.										
2. Learn about the relationship between appropriate and inappropriate physical contact.				x						
3. Learn about the relationship between rules, laws, safety and the protection of individual rights.										
4. Demonstrate the ability to assert boundaries, rights and personal privacy.			x	x	x					
5. Identify resource people in the school and community and how to seek support and help.	x									
6. Apply effective problem-solving and decision-making skills to make safe and healthy choices.										
7. Learn about the physical and emotional damages of alcohol and other drug use and abuse.										x
8. Learn techniques for handling stress and coping with conflict to manage life events.										

A Note From Connie

This book has been a labor of love. In it I've shared my favorite activities.

For over 20 years I have been working with students of all ages — elementary through college — and the lessons in these pages represent my work with them. Of the many things I've done in the counseling and education field, I've always found the direct contact with students to be the most rewarding, exciting and challenging. The repertoire of activities that I've developed over the years has been an important part of my effectiveness. I've been asked many times to share my activities with others, and now I'm pleased to have finally written a book that contains some of my favorites.

Through the years, I have used all of these activities with students of virtually all ages. Some activities may seem more appropriate for older students and others may seem written for the younger ones. However, with some modification, change of language, and examples, most activities can work with most any audience. I encourage you to adapt the activities to fit your style and the abilities of your students.

I would like to hear from you about how you are using these lessons. I care about your success and wish you the best. I am available for consultation and to do workshops. I look forward to hearing from you and will be happy to respond to any questions you have.

Connie Messina

References and Resources

Armstrong, Thomas. 1995. *The Myth of the A.D.D. Child*. New York, NY: Penguin Books.

Batmanghelidj, F. 1999. *Your Body's Many Cries For Water*. Falls Church, VA: Global Health Solutions, Inc.

Buzan, Tony. 1991. *Use Both Sides of Your Brain*. New York, NY: Penguin Books USA.

Campbell, Chari and Dahir, Carol. 1997. *The National Standards for School Counseling Programs*. Alexandria, VA: American School Counselor Association.

Carnegie, Dale. 1937. *How To Win Friends and Influence People*. NY, NY: Simon & Schuster.

Cavanaugh, Brian. 1998. *Sower's Seeds of Encouragement*. Mahwah, New Jersey: Paulist Press.

Corcoran, John. 1994. *The Teacher Who Couldn't Read*. Colorado Springs, CO: Focus on The Family.

DePorter, Bobbi, Reardon, Mark; Singer-Nourie, Sarah. *Quantum Teaching*. 1999. Needham Heights, Ma: Allyn & Bacon

Fankhauser, Jerry. 1980. *From A Chicken to An Eagle*. Farmingdale, NY: Coleman Publishing.

Goleman, Daniel. 1995. *Emotional Intelligence: Why It Can Matter More Than IQ*. New York, NY: Bantam Books.

Hall, Calvin and Nordby, Vernon. 1973. *A Primer of Jungian Psychology*. Markham, Ontario: Penguin Books Canada Limited.

Jampolsky, Gerald. 1979. *Love Is Letting Go of Fear*. Berkeley, CA: Celestial Arts.

Jensen, Eric. 2000. *Brain-Based Learning*. 1995. *The Learning Brain*. 1988. *Super Teaching*. San Diego, CA: The Brain Store Publishing.

Kohl, Robert. 1991. *I won't Learn From You*. Minneapolis, Minn: Milkweed Editions.

Kuykendall, Crystal. 1992. *From Rage To Hope: Strategies for Reclaiming Black And Hispanic Students*. Bloomington, Indiana: National Educational Service.

Lindamood-Bell Learning Processses. (800) 233-1819.

Nerburn, Kent, Editor. 1999. *The Wisdom of The Native Americans*. Novato, CA: New World Library.

Neskahi, Arlan. *From Anger Management to Anger Resolution.* An unplublished Curriculum Website: www.rainbowwalker.com/anger

Padus, Emrika. 1992. *The Complete Guide To Your Emotions and Your Health.* Rodale, PA, Rodale Press.

Palomares, Susanna, and Cowan, David. 1996. *50 Activities for Teaching Emotional Intelligence.* Carson, CA: Innerchoice Publishing.

Peace Pilgrim. 1982. *Peace Pilgrim: Her Life and Work In Her Own Words.* USA: Friends of Peace Pilgrim.

Pert, Candace. 1997. *Molecules of Emotion.* New York, NY: Scribner

Roger, John and McWilliams, Peter. 1994. *You Can't Afford The Luxury of a Negative Thought.* Los Angeles, CA: Prelude Press.

Sheldon, Carolyn. ———. *E.Q. in School Counseling.* Carson, CA: Innerchoice Publishing.

Sousa, David. 2000. *How The Brain Learns.* Thousand Oaks, CA: Corwin Press.

The Learning Forum, "Suppercamp." (800) 285-3276.

Vos, Jeannette and Dryden, Gordon. 1999. *The Learning Revolution.* Torrance, CA: The Learning Web.

White, Anne Terry, Editor. 1969. *Aesop's Fables.* Sacramento, CA: California State Department of Education.

CPSIA information can be obtained at www.ICGtesting.com
Printed in the USA
BVOW041709021011

272599BV00001B/12/P